THE NEW
MYTHOLOGIES

NEW PSALMS FOR A NEW WORLD

THE NEW MYTHOLOGIES

NEW PSALMS FOR A NEW WORLD

JAYCE DALTON FREE

White Falcon Publishing

The New Mythologies
Jayce Dalton Free

Published by White Falcon Publishing,
Chandigarh, India

ISBN - 979-8-89222-423-9

Table of Contents

INTRODUCTION

There is a God in whom I believe, yet whose very existence I quite often question openly and entirely. This non-physical 'God', though invisible and silent, seems, on occasion, as real as any other aspect of reality. Sometimes, I feel a closeness to this undefinable underlying presence – a force that I cannot *rationally* confirm to any other person (nor at times to myself).

To this unseen presence, perhaps within or perhaps without, I feel a perennially enduring connection – although at times waxing, at times waning. It is a unique form of relationship – longer lasting and more deeply meaningful than any other relationship I have ever had. And while I have several conversations each day with other *actual people*, my subconscious dialogue between this greater entity and myself is nearly constant - whether I deem it as so or not.

On a superficial level, we could say that I 'believe' in this underlying entity who does not *insist* that I believe in him. Almost ambivalent at times, he allows, and even facilitates, our varied thoughts and manners of operation within this world. It seems he might not even care so much whether or not I 'believe' in 'him'. He seems to prefer endowing and enabling us with unbridled consciousness, thereby allowing and entrusting us to navigate events and conditions correctly – at least within this physical world, wherein we humans abide. And when we fail, as it is certain that we will, he is unfailingly resilient in tolerance and absolution – for the flow of our conscious presence in this world is unbroken, unfettered, and unbounded.

But 'beliefs' aside, to some extent, my consciousness (and each individual's consciousness) could be seen as an extension of that greater, more permeating, yet formless 'form' of consciousness; for it is not by any act of my *own* will that the *fundamental* nature of my own awareness arises. While I exert some control over the direction and subject of my thoughts, neither I nor science can adequately define or explain the *underlying nature* of consciousness. Consciousness, of the type I regularly experience, goes *far beyond* any mechanistic definition that has ever been provided or espoused.

In one manner of speaking, a pre-conscious matrix of a type we can't fully comprehend seemingly prefabricates or predefines some characteristics or parameters of our very essence (that internal essence, being, or soul).

Within this construct, a primordial form of preconsciousness provides the basis by which our human *type* of consciousness may exist. This type of consciousness seemingly arises from, but is inarguably tethered to, the physical world in such a way that we can experience and act upon the material aspect of the universe. This great coupling of consciousness with materiality, Life, is a state or commodity highly sought and valued by the Eternal Essence – a miraculous achievement, a sparkling gem, a brightly shining star.

While this 'God', I believe, revels in and indulges Life's individuation and the related formalization of thought, he is also quite accessible for a more intensified and attuned connection – a rather more personal (yet still esoteric) connection.

We are, without any effort at all, 'one with God' in many respects. But there are additional *states* in which this connection between a greater form of consciousness (God) and any one of its discrete entities (a human, for example) is not disdained, disregarded, or broken, but instead becomes heightened, harmonious, intertwined, and enhanced. God, in this light, can be our friend, our constant companion, and we can be his useful and powerful Atman or Avatar in *this* world.

Certainly, some will roll their eyes in incredulity at these notions, and I *might* too - depending on my mood when hearing of such ideas. But perhaps we *might* pause to experience, or at least consider, the great joy and sense of calm oneness that may occur within these enhanced or empowered states.

Perhaps it is but a fantasy, but are not some fantasies worth indulging? And are not some perceived realities as *nearly* real (at least to the beholder) as those literally or more formally experienced?

On the other hand, perhaps there *is*, in fact, a conscious force underlying, encompassing, and perhaps predating all reality. Do we know with certainty that there is not? And is it not possible that we are a part of, or an extension of, that greater consciousness? Perhaps we are discrete conscious 'objects' derived from a class or construct known as 'consciousness'?

Perhaps we are even upon the leading edge of a great and meaningful unfolding in this grand process which we call *Life*.

For the moment, perhaps we can put aside our stereotypical notions of 'God'. In doing so, let's set aside our own notions that he is 'perfect' according to our own limited definitions of 'perfect'. Let's set aside the idea that he must 'live up to' our own humanly and simplistic notions of perfection; *all*-good, *all*-knowing, or *all*-powerful. Our notions regarding 'perfection' are, in fact, 'imperfect'. In order to *be* God, God does not *have to be* any of these things, nor must he fit into any of our limited ideas concerning these overused and overarching superlatives.

For the moment, consider all of reality as being more or less of a reflection or emanation of an underlying form of consciousness which we might call 'God' - along with all that *we* deem good and bad - perfect and imperfect. And along with those notions, let's set aside the notion that God is unyieldingly static; for the very notion of 'creation' implies change and 'newness'.

Perhaps we should also assume that, in some small measure, as seems apparent from observing the undeniable reality in which we live, we *do* have some influence on the present moment and upon its outcome, and perhaps even some bearing upon what 'should be' versus what perhaps 'should not be'. Our actions and sentiments, as living beings constituted by a conscious God, do actually matter; and perhaps we can have an impact in ways beyond what we can currently imagine.

On a deeper level, many of our internal conflicts represent or symbolize the ancient conceptual conflicts which stirred within the primordial. Resolving some of life's conflicts or problems in a *favorable* manner certainly may have a great impact upon us individually. But perhaps in resolving deeper and greater issues, there is even some impact on those aged, shared conflicts on a much higher yet more fundamental level.

Realize, most importantly, it is not without purpose that we exist, and our actions *can* clearly change our own localized conditions somewhat dramatically. In a more substantial way, we each contribute to the whole, wherein the net effects of our collective actions *do* have great and considerable impacts upon the course of both physical and metaphysical outcomes.

THE NATURE OF THIS WORK

As is appropriate to the subject matter, the language, wording, and style of this volume are of a somewhat symbolic and inspired nature. In light of this, '*The New Mythologies*' does not attempt to be overly scholarly or worldly. As such, it is representative of a voice that is, at times, somewhat spiritual in tone. It is not *deliberately* philosophical and, as such, does not *always* intend to sway or convince the reader of the logical validity of principles or ideas – but rather it often simply states them flatly and without precondition.

It does attempt to portray, in raw form, certain inspired or inspirational feelings. It attempts to pursue certain ideals and other empowering feelings with abandon, and to their ultimate and unobstructed conclusions. Here we will pursue 'the Ultimate' quite linearly, with a minimum of detracting lateral distraction or obfuscating cross-examination. Those types of philosophical querying and deconstruction would largely reside in other separate volumes.

As with all ideals and higher aspirations, I must admit that I do not always adhere to the principles espoused, and in some measure, I have failed to do so *despite* my best intentions. But we must always understand that human error and personal failings do not invalidate the ideas and ideals themselves.

*The setbacks we suffer and the limitations with which we are saddled do not negate nor significantly detract from the validity of our highest aspirations – nor are the **best** of our observations and expressions negated by the lesser among them.*

Dedication

This book is dedicated to that pre-conscious source of all things, and the physicalized embodiment of all that is; the consciousness from which our own awareness is derived, or by which it is composed and thus, in turn, composes. This essence to which I dedicate this book, without any degree of pun or sarcasm, is that which we might call 'God'.

Beyond this dedication, many portions were directly written *to* that entity or *for* that greater force. While the Greater Consciousness exists beyond mere words, our words serve to focus and channel our thoughts. Our thoughts, in turn, color and direct our consciousness, which can then become more attuned toward the greater and finer aspects of Life, wherein on a deeper level, we can harmonize more closely with Greater Consciousness. This is the ideal toward which many psalms and prayers are raised – to engage with a keener degree of closeness with God.

Not to or for myself or others, many of the psalms herein are directed and spoken to or for this ever-living consciousness. While others (and myself in recollection) may benefit from considering these passages, and *some* were indeed written for clarification toward any potential 'human' readers, there are, obviously, some passages that are meant as praise or recognition toward the Creator-Sustainer.

But we, in observing and reflecting upon these passages, I hope, may benefit to some extent by broadening our understanding and passion towards Life and all that it comprises. Thus, this dedication to the conscious creative force within and behind reality is, in turn, a dedication toward *all* consciousness and all that has been created, i.e., Life, that most beloved and manifold creation.

A MIRACLE WITNESSING A MIRACLE

A baby Eskimo clings tightly to her mother as they emerge from their igloo into the cold night air. As she looks upward toward the ever-darkened sky, she sees a snowflake falling – drifting slowly through the crisp, clear ether. It is silhouetted perfectly against the blackness as it passes just before her wide-open eyes. In a world of snow, it is at this moment that she really notices a *single* snowflake for the first time.

For the first time, she giggles aloud as something leaps within her - awakened by this sight.

Now awakened, she becomes a *conscious* witness to the unfolding miracle of all that is.

So, we might ask, does that one snowflake in a sky full of snowflakes hold any real meaning at all?

Well, I will give you *my* simple answer, "Yes, it does for her."

A STARCHILD AND ONE WITH GOD

We are...

One with God.

One with the Universe.

Each of us...

A Star Child - Made of Stardust.

A Child of the Most High God.

A miracle witnessing a miracle.

We are children of God.

Made in the Image of God.

(Love yourself as such, treat yourself as such.)

My energy is one with the Universe,

A Star-child, my physical body is made of the physical stuff of the stars.

A child of God, my consciousness is made of the conscious matter of God.

A miracle witnessing a miracle from within.

The miracle of consciousness witnessing the ongoing miracle of creation.

The miracle of awareness immersed within and participating in the miracle of physical reality.

A Miracle by
Any Other Name

Science can trace origins through layer upon layer, eon upon eon - piecing together a rather astonishing historical cosmology. Particles arise spontaneously, in mass, across seemingly infinite positions throughout an infinite volume of space. These particles, due to various laws of physics, coalesce and form stars and planets and *all* the physical substances that we know. On through the momentous arising of life from raw matter, we eventually see the emergence of enumerable fantastical lifeforms. And ultimately there arise lifeforms capable of a keen awareness of all things including a growing knowledge of this great unfolding to which they themselves are a party.

Can a greater tale than this be told? Can a greater miracle than this be imagined?

Surely, reality is stranger than fiction.

While science can trace the origins of one thing back to a prior source, each 'source' is but another derived 'thing'. At the fringe of it all, there is always complete uncertainty. No matter how deeply we 'know', another question always underlies.

At the very essence of our knowledge, and underlying our very existence, lies the unanswerable question, "How can everything or anything exist?"

Whether created by a god or by some rationalized random accident, it still begs the question, "How do we get something from nothing?"

Science can break everything down into smaller and smaller particles, but how did those particles get there? Did they just 'pop in' to existence, or did they mysteriously arrive from somewhere else? The Big Bang may have occurred as scientists have theoretically deduced, but how did the vast quantities of matter initially form that caused it? There had to be a 'ginormous' volume of particles predating the Big Bang, and even one particle is *something*. Where did it come from? Did everything just spontaneously arise? That would *surely* be classified as a miracle.

And yet, if God created everything, then what created God? Did God make himself? Or did another God make him, and then who made that God? And so on.

Why would *anything*, let alone *everything*, just happen to exist? Yet it does, and it does so in grand fashion.

Everything, in all of its exquisite variation, *does* exist beyond our wildest dreams.

In one sense, ***reality defies reality.***

The existence of everything is illogical. Yet it is undeniable and therefore miraculous.

The farther we look into space, the more we see its unlimited expansiveness. This process *seems* to expand the size of the 'known' universe. However, the 'known' universe is only the portion known to us, or more accurately, that portion ever so slightly comprehended by only a few of us.

We know that each star is like a sun, and many of them are capable of having life-bearing planets in tow. There are known to be more stars in our own galaxy than there are people on Earth, and there are more *galaxies* in the universe than there are people on Earth. We can multiply the number of stars by the number of galaxies to get an inkling of the vast number of potential suns in the known universe.

And each day, with our increased ability to see more deeply into space, we discover more. Always more.

So, there is every reason to believe that we have only seen a thimbleful (of space) in an allegorical ocean. And this universe may be but one of an infinite number of universes.

Likewise, why does time exist? Without time, there can be no change. If time did not always exist, nothing could have changed into something from some perpetually frozen state of nothingness. And yet, why would time itself exist, and why would *anything* exist, even those esoteric 'things' like time, gravity, or thought? But those 'esoteric' things are quite real too, are they not?

If created by a god, who and what created him, and *why* would he (or it) just exist?

And why would such a conscious entity create such a vast universe of universes?

> ***The existence of anything and everything is a miracle.***

We are living within a miracle, whether randomly and spontaneously arising against all odds or even more miraculous if spun into existence by some vast super-conscious entity. Some may prefer not to call it a miracle, but a miracle is still a miracle, even by any other name.

And if God were pure consciousness alone before materiality was 'invented', *how* does consciousness manifest the material? And philosophically, we might ask, "Why?"

On the other hand, if dead materiality existed without cause (and this too is completely illogical), *why* would it, and how could it, develop consciousness and awareness of the type we so clearly and dearly know? For matter to develop a form of consciousness that is aware of itself; *Why* would it? This too is a philosophical question one should deeply query before accepting as 'known' all other scientific explanations, regardless of how plausible they may be.

If all has arisen from consciousness, then all form may be but a perceived reality within the vast consciousness of God. All of us, you and I, perhaps but figures in a dream of sorts.

But if life is but a dream, it is such a convincing dream that we might as well call this dream 'Reality'. The origin of this reality does not diminish its 'realness' – the very hard yet supple nature of a physical reality blended with conscious awareness.

So, the ultimate questions remain unanswered – and certainly, the entirety of our knowledge of reality is held within these greater questions – bounding, underlying, and foreshadowing *all* things and circumscribing all that we *think* we know. And in witnessing this miracle from within, it seems that these greater questions may remain unanswered and may, in practicality, be unanswerable.

Yet science seems quite clear about one thing – our physical bodies (and all that is physical in our world) are made of molecules whose core 'parts' (atoms and subatomic particles) came into existence at the 'beginning' of this known universe. All of it, everything, is essentially stardust. The very material that completely makes up our bodies is as old as the universe itself, and all of it came from stars.

For me, it is nice to know that we are children of the stars, from the heavens, if you will.

> ***Each of us is a Star-Child, consisting of a fabric as old as the universe.***

Matter is energy, according to science, and so we too are made of energy. Stardust is physical matter, and all physical matter is simply another form of energy when observed at the molecular level. Even though matter to us seems 'solid' or hard, it is, in fact, a form of energy that may be considered rather ethereal or formless in some respects.

Furthermore, it seems that consciousness is *also* a type of energy. Consciousness is indeed a *very different type* of energy, one that will never be strictly defined in terms of matter and particles.

Many religions tell us that we are the 'children' of God, made in his image. Perhaps the deeper meaning of this is lost by many. 'Made in the image of God' does not mean that God is a primate and he created us to physically resemble him. The concept of 'made in the image of God' does not refer so much to the physical form of our bodies, but rather to that innermost piece of consciousness or awareness.

The Soul, as we may call it (some have called it the Atman, or even the Thetan), is that conscious part of us which is 'made in the image of God' (Greater Consciousness). It does not really matter so much what we call it – the soul, the self, the awareness; it is a conscious being with awareness. The awareness that we have is like a smaller but more refined piece of the greater awareness. It is like a reflection of the Greater Consciousness. It is thus our *soul* and our consciousness that is 'made in the image of God'.

It is in this way that we are said to be 'Children of God'; that our **souls** are made of his primordial conscious energy in the same way that our **bodies** consist of particle energies that arose at the dawn of the universe.

Within this understanding - the understanding that there will be no *absolute* understanding - there is the realization that all things reside within a universe of unknown and almost unimaginable origin and scope. Thus, it is my belief, and suffice it to say, that we are indeed ourselves miracles, witnessing a miraculous universe from within. This fact, for the individual, overshadows in relevance *all* the analytical knowledge, which might or might not ever be known or knowable.

From that uniquely amazing vantage point, we are not merely passive entities, but we are also actively participating *within* this miraculous universe. We each exert the bearing and direction of our own consciousness to some extent, and we collectively exert the influence of Greater Consciousness upon the physical universe, en masse.

The above seems more resolute and, in my estimation, more reliable than most other findings - a conclusion, though vague, of the utmost relevance. Ironically, this *vagueness* accurately reflects the nature of reality, or the position within it where we reside. This uncertainty, when expressed accurately, conveys the ultimate malleability inherent within the universe of the future.

For it is a conclusion that does not ascertain the origin of things any more than those origins can ever be accurately apprehended or fully fathomed. However, it does speak volumes to our perceptions regarding our *position* within our reality in the present. Moreover, it alludes to the notion that *we*, along with a Greater Consciousness, can and do exert a perpetual influence upon the unfolding of the future by our combined and very conscious existence. We are parts of that Greater Consciousness, and what we think, believe, and *do*, in an ongoing way, exerts some degree of influence. And in this way, what we do, say, think, and believe – all of these, in some ways, do indeed matter.

Certainly, outside of the context of a greater consciousness and a greater universe, this idea also asserts that what we think, believe, and do *really* matter;

if nothing else, to us (individually and collectively). In the same way that a single falling snowflake *does* matter to an Eskimo girl on a cold Alaskan evening – all the details of Life, which we are a party to, *do*, in fact, matter to us. And our reactions to these things matter to us individually and to those around us as well.

Aside from the values inherent within the assertions already made (concerning the elevated value of consciousness in the miraculous present *and* the influence of consciousness upon the present and future), we may wish to speculate further about origins and the past. While this may not be as important as we seem to believe, nevertheless, I will attempt to entertain further speculation.

The 'best' summary is that a primordial 'god' existed, having consciousness (a form of energy) of a different type and magnitude than we do, and who has, for reasons lost to time, manifested himself into the physical universe as we know it. Thus, he divests a part of himself into discrete elements of consciousness (like ourselves). Evolving, as it were (for lack of a better term), through various stages of life throughout the universe as we know it (and well beyond everything that we know).

> **Wonderful it is that God so wanted to become each of us.**

But the *knowledge* of absolute certainties concerning ancient origins and the makings of all things is highly overrated – at least compared to the knowledge of the position of our awareness in the *now*. In practicality, the knowledge of the place and relevance of our awareness is much more important and useful, as is our role in ushering in a better future for ourselves and our collective reality via our actions taken perpetually within the present.

And somewhat sad it is too, when we squander this incredible awareness of the fact that we are one with God and children of the Most High. We too often forget that we are made in the image of his consciousness. We often forget that God wished to become us, or that his conscious emanations would one day arise as the very human lifeforms that we embody today.

Here again, 'made in his image' does not (as the simpleton believes) mean that 'God' has two arms and two legs. Very obviously, it means that our core consciousness, our soul, contains an element of Life – God-given consciousness. Thus, we are given and animated by a small reflection or embodiment of a greater consciousness that is highly exalted.

The individual 'self' is a more focused and individuated instance of a more fundamental and primordial *type* of consciousness. Just as the stardust that composes our bodies is as old as the universe, we are not actually 'stars'. Similarly, our consciousness is derived from

God, but is not literally the same as God. So we are made of the eternal matter of the universe – stardust, and we are made in the *image* of a God, Greater Consciousness, but we are not literally 'God'.

Creation, as it is, may seem imperfect to us, and its origins may have arguably been more greatly so. It may be observed that across whichever path the universe has evolved, it did so from a place that was decidedly more chaotic in its origin. Perhaps creating an entire universe is not as easy or straightforward as it seems. We perceive many imperfections and problems, many of which we must endure. But *all* is to the credit of the Greater Consciousness, and perhaps it is toward the conclusion of all things, rather than from its uncertain beginnings, that is destined for a 'perfect' resolution. As all things will be honed by the consciousness, of which each of us is a part, toward a progressive resolution that is by some standards 'more perfect' as defined and then refined by all aspects of Greater Consciousness, thus there is 'purpose' even in our recognition of brokenness.

Thus, the inevitable refinement of all things in accordance with the conscious principle of the universe may be deemed an irreversible act of limitless perfection, the end of which may be seen as 'paradise' or 'heaven'. Along the way, we must be forgiving of the process from which all things arose, and in recognition of the chaos from which things were born. In this way, we must be forgiving of one another, of creation, and especially of the creator. For his perfection lies not in the past but perhaps in the future.

These are my beliefs, though the certainty of many of these may be fairly debated. However, the certainty that we are miraculous entities consciously participating in a miraculous existence can scarcely be questioned. And clearly, we have some choice in matters, and we have at least some effects on the outcome of at least some things. And I, for one, consider this a very good thing.

The God of
Superseding Superlatives

You are the God of superseding superlatives.

All thought and word derive from you, so no word for you is unfitting; yet any word falls far short.

In my adoration of you and your creation, I will often call upon you by many creative or descriptive names and titles.

The names often used in addressing you, such as 'Oh Lord', 'My God', or 'Holy Spirit', while common and acceptable, are yet nonspecific and perhaps lacking in appropriate color and splendor. The vague or lacking imagery invoked by these traditional 'names' or titles perhaps fails to convey the power and vitality of your many dimensions.

In our focused human physical forms, we are often only capable of seeing and understanding small facets of you and your miraculous creation. So, by recognizing more of your many faces and qualities, we can perhaps more genuinely come to appreciate *all* that you are, all that you have done, and all that you will do.

I believe that the practice of addressing you using more creative names or titles, tied with descriptive adjectives, deepens our connection and more accurately honors you and all of your magnificent creations. This is a practice that can broaden our understanding of your multi-faceted nature.

If it were not so, would you not have me say it?

In your incalculable name,

Amen

ALL PRAISE THE ULTIMATE

All praise the Ultimate, beyond words yet the mother of all words. Within and behind all words and their meanings. Embracing yet escaping meaning, which extends so far beyond words. Predating *all* meaning and far surpassing the meanings of any mere words.

The father of words not yet spoken; the origin of a thousand thoughts heretofore unknown.

"Behold, I am doing a *new* thing!", and within this utterance was spun the multiverse.

Thank you, Master of All, for humbling us with your awe, and yet bestowing upon us a form of greatness, all our own.

Thrilled are we to be chief among your designs for your newest manifestations.

For now, I will behold all with a heightened sense of wonderment, as we will be centrally engrossed within your next most surpassing evolvement.

The world and all the universe, clad in all its golden-stardust-splendor – will be yet far surpassed by the *new thing* which you have set in motion before me.

We might call it *heaven* or *paradise*, but the grandeur of your greatest iteration is only limited by these simple notions.

It is with joy, exalted and excited, that I rise to this occasion. With uncontained exuberance, I will gladly be a party, strongly unto it.

Casting aside my forlorn ways and broken notions, I realign – and emboldened, see the culmination of *better* things awaiting.

Ablaze and aglow, former limitations are shed like shackles broken.

Ignited, like clockwork, your seals will be faithfully executed in the manner of their intended effects. And in your due time, all that is manifest will come to pass.

Your testing and proving are just and in good measure. Thus, all things without, and all things within, which are counted as 'less than' shall fall and fade away. And that which is good, and wholesome, and kind, and joyous, and prosperous, and worthy - these will remain. And this righteous cleaving alone would be of magnanimous result, yet to that which is remaining so much more will be added and multiplied.

The Ultimate, beyond that which we cannot perceive, far surpasses the awesome yet chaotic nature from which we arose, and will yet retain in best form *all* that which might *best* survive and thrive.

In no context abiding by your careful comparison will the failed succeed.

Nor with your feeling will pain endure.
With your courage never will fear prevail.
With your wisdom never confusion and chaos may reign.
With your kindness will hatred fall.
And against your true goodness, evil flickers and fades.

Forging the new with nimble amassed, by your sight I see now what I cannot see.
I will be what I cannot be.
Beyond what I am now, I will behold all things anew as a traveler in a strange new land.

To live always happy, joyous, and forever healthy, in this state I thank you. Gleaming in each moment, unperturbed by the possibility of malevolence.

The malaise and disease that had plagued us, forever now obliterated by our dominion over them. Such will be that by a simple flick of the wrist or twinkling of an eye, we will dispel these 'demons' that once plagued us for eons, or for a season.

For we fully know not your feelings and volitions since they are beyond our own. Though ancient and expansive, they are precursors to our awareness. That which you have encountered and sifted through to bestow upon us in the now, and in the right time, for this we are forever thankful – though this too is something that we can scarcely begin to comprehend.

All praise the Ultimate, the source, the perseverant, the rapturous.

All praise, that we, in our way of thinking, might begin to understand yours. All praise that we might see beyond our own suffering and appreciate yours. All praise, in that you have allowed us to come to this moment – and that you, around us, within us, and *as* us, hear us and allow us fair and reasonable bearing upon the course of all events.

All praise and thanks for that which we are, and more so for that which we will become.

And praise, for all that has come before, *especially* all that which has been along the good and best path.

In all these ways, and for all these ways, and more,

I give praise and thanks.

Standing awake in thrilled and eager anticipation.

Amen, Amen.

QUESTIONS OVER NOTIONS OF GOD

We are told to believe in God, but what does that really mean?

What does it really mean to 'believe'? And how does one do so?

Do we not simply believe what we believe, or are we expected to *make* ourselves 'believe' in something that we cannot, in good conscience, feel strongly about?

Why does it matter?

Can belief not follow reason and observation rather than merely acting as a pre-filter upon any new thought or idea encountered?

Does God dislike these questions?

What is this God we 'must' believe in?

And 'must' we believe him to be a very specific way, even though we cannot possibly comprehend him?

What is he like? What is he *really* like? Or perhaps more 'it' than 'he'.

If he exists, what *might* he be?

Is it wrong to ponder and query over what God might be like?

The New Mythologies

Can I truly believe in something I have only superficially defined or beheld?
Can I, in the name of honesty, attest to something I do not know?
Does God then not want us to seek him?
Can I seek without wishing to know?
Can I seek to know without delving and questioning?

Am I only to know something from the comfort of my easy chair?

To know God, we must reflect upon God. With questions and openness alike, we must make some *effort* before claiming that we know.
We must seek, or else how can we find?

DISCERNMENT AND ACCEPTANCE

Discernment is the act of making comparisons among differing things or ideas. Ideally, when we use our innate faculties of discernment, we are seeking the better option among two or more different conclusions. We must often discern among different courses of action – and in doing so, we try to evaluate which will yield the best possible outcomes.

The strength of one's powers of discernment may be a strong measure of intelligence, and this trait is likely what has allowed the human species to prevail over so many challenges and adversities.

We strengthen our powers of discernment by *using* them - by *exercising* them. Use them, when applicable, in as many creative ways as possible. The strength and creativeness of your power to discern, and how often you choose to exercise it, may well determine your degree of success in many endeavors. Perhaps this may ultimately determine your degree of success in life – regardless of how you define success.

At each juncture, we must often reevaluate. Each answer must be, in turn, questioned. Even the strongest plan must be tested, and the test itself must be tested.

Even spiritual topics and ideas concerning the nature of Reality and God must be given careful and honest scrutiny from every angle. Why would we not use our powers of discernment regarding the more important topics instead of only the trivial?

But there is also a time to give the mind its rest. A time to refrain from judgment or comparisons. A time to step back and view anything and everything with acceptance. There is a time for, and some value to, an accepting sense of appreciation. There is a power and a joy that comes with acceptance.

A flow state may result from a generalized attitude of acceptance coupled with a somewhat detached state – a state in which we accept the messy uncertainties inherent within all things. A flow state is quite magical, as are the related states of meditation and mindfulness – yet the flow state is quite a different state from these. Within the flow state, things seem to occur naturally or fluidly, and everything seems to be occurring exactly as it is supposed to be.

Taking a broader view, our three most positive mental states can be seen as:

- Reflexive Mindfulness – this is primarily a state of awareness coupled with discernment in which questions are freely encouraged to arise. It is the basis of critical thought, evaluation, vision, and planning. It is primarily a thought state.

- Appreciative Calm – a relaxed, appreciative state of acceptance. This can be a state of relaxation, meditation, or recreational diversion. It is primarily an emotional or spiritual state.

- Active Flow State – a state in which activities seem effortless or enhanced, and everything seems to occur fluidly and with great precision or effectiveness. This is a 'get it done' state, or an idealized work state. It is primarily a physical state but combines elements of the other two states in balance.

Outside of these, or any other beneficial or joyous states, most of our mental states can be seen as somewhat negative or detractive. If a mental state is neither enjoyable nor productive, what value can it possibly have? (Although sometimes a nagging negative emotion is there to alert us that something is wrong.)

More aptly, if the wheels of mental machinery are mostly making noise, we may need to tune it more finely. Or, for a greater refactoring, we may need to reset and 'let go'. View all from afar and in a somewhat detached manner – as if from 'outside the box'. Then stay in that state until a more certain, beneficial, or joyous train of thought arises.

In short, do not be blindly driven by incessant thoughts and judgments. Rather, at times, refrain from them, so as to let them pass in quiet observation. And at other times, rather than being driven by your own thoughts and judgments, strive instead to proactively *drive* your thoughts into realms that you find either enjoyable or productive.

If a train of thought is bringing you no joy and no positive results, then stop engaging with it. Or if it seems necessary, find a way to engage with it in a state of joyous acceptance or detachment. Even better, find *another* pursuit or train of thought that better suits you and brings you peace, love, happiness, or joy. Find a pursuit or focus that brings you closer to something you personally value or with which you resonate – or something that has some obvious value or virtue above and beyond yourself.

Remember that despite external influences and habitually fortified patterns, you are ultimately in control of your thought-life, and your mental state, and as such, are largely responsible for them.

It is best to apply some degree of discernment in these, as in all matters.

THE MASTER OF THE LIGHT AND THE DARK

You are the master of the light that pierces the dark; a thousand pinpoints piercing the infinite; pulsing, aglow, beaming, peering eternally outward. You are the origin of the brilliance that is light.

By day, glowing with vivid colors – revealing all forms to the eye. Moreover, you are the eye and the soul by which the eye sees. For what is the eye that can be explained by scientists and sages? Is it like a camera, as they say?

No, it is the camera that is like the eye. And it is neither the eye nor the camera, but the *being within* that ultimately becomes aware and makes use of all manner of imagery.

And to describe this as a mere process of reflection and refraction is to sheerly run amiss of the true magic of vision. For the seer, the beholder, and the conscious soul that sees; this being so endowed is far above and beyond a mere technical process.

You, the Brilliant, are wavelength and frequency. You illuminate and radiate across the spectrum, and you reside at the very source and origin of all these phenomena, not only predating and presiding over the physical properties themselves, but also originating the very concept of these phenomena.

Moreover, you are the eye, and more importantly, you give life underlying to the soul into which vision occurs.

You are the origin of the power of the word. Wondrous power is in words, and you are their grand master. You are the waveform and vibration, and yet you are the ear that hears and discerns with understanding. From thunders to whispers, you are the precursor to all – both the sound and the listener.

The spoken word conveys, in an instant, the entirety of a notion in all its depth and subtlety of variation. A tree can be many things, but the single word conveys them all in their variances. And you, almighty, are the origin of words and meanings, and you have imbued each of us with this innate ability.

The ear, magnificent as it is, can be described as a mechanism that detects variances in sonic frequency and pressure. But this does not begin to explain how the soulful mind perceives and derives meaning from words. Each word represents a primordial archetype, the knowing of which is an innate power of *You*, my almighty source and maker. This power of knowing words, forms, and meanings, you have embedded within us. Most thankful we are that sounds can make words, and words can have meanings, and these meanings we can observe and command by the sheer and effortless power of *words*.

And among the many illustrious titles, you are also the Dimensioner of Space and Time. Spanning and underlying all that is, you are the matrix from which all things arise. Both things and events among things – and of interactions – for without time, there is no change, and nothing can be different from one moment to the next. Without time, nothing can be, for to have something in one moment from nothing in a previous moment implies time – without which all change or newness is impossible.

Above all, you are the God of the New, for you revel in creation as we are awed within it. Putting into space all things, and before that the notion of each thing, and before that the notion of things in general. And before that, time, and the notion of time, which is the notion of things interacting with one another and changing over time. Forming endlessly newer 'things', arising from their iterative events, and progressively bringing forth all new and superior forms and ever more spectacular events.

Almighty Creator, be assured, that at least the best of your creation smiles back at you - as you gleam and shine above, within, and betwixt it all. For who, but you, can swim amidst all parts of all things, imbuing space with ever more polished and constructive forms. Yet stitching always with skilled craft, each moment to the next, thus endlessly ensuring that the context of our conscious reality remains unbroken and ever-flowing.

Joy increases with each iteration, or nearly so. And each change and each new thing, against your just testing, and judging by ours, produces even more brilliant results. The unfolding of Life in space and time is the grand reflection of your brilliance and grandeur.

And even in gravity, your design reigns supreme. In such a simple thing, while we are yet able to quantify and measure, we are still at a loss to fully define or explain its true cause. The genius of our scientists and sages has yet to fully understand this simple feature, but only through mere formulas and observations.

The origin of gravity is indeed another fundamental within your subtle sustaining splendor. In it, and with it, we may stand erect and walk about. That we may amble, stride, and roll about in every manner of vehicle and thereby partake of a reality of this uniquely Terran nature, which is so welcoming and familiar to us – such is one of your keenest yet often overlooked designs. Not in and of itself alone that it is so wondrous, but more so, in that it yields the type of habitat and structure within which our human reality primarily transpires.

And while our scholars cannot fully grasp it intellectually, you, Almighty One, have given each of us the simple and true understanding of gravity.

This understanding of gravity which you gave us, lies within our own feet.

> All praise the Master Builder
> and Sustainer of all that is,
> was, and ever will be
> 'new'.

> Amen

PRAYER FOR THE EVER UNFOLDING

Prayer for the Ever Unfolding of the New and Wondrous Things:

Thank you, my dearest friend, the Almighty Creator, for all that is, and more so for the splendor of all that is coming. I know, my Lord, my Guide, that in your due time and in well-tested and careful ways, all the coming 'newness' will far surpass in sheer magnificence all that in its unequaled grandeur is the now.

For I know that you love doing a new thing, a greater thing, and a better thing – always.

And only with you is a *truly* new thing even possible, for without you, *no* 'thing' or event is possible. Nothing is possible without you. If that which is, was once new, then indeed, with you, God, at any time, a truly *new* universe may come to pass. Or the old may be altered in any dramatically new way, even in the twinkling of an eye.

This is an amazing power which, God, you have; to make a new thing, a new concept, a new design. An improvement, a radical alteration. Any change that suits you, the unfolding evolution of the universe is fashioned and directed by you. Yes, you, the maker and sustainer, may guide and change the course of all. Standing outside the boundaries of all, and likewise from within, you fluidly morph the greater and personal realities.

Thank you, Great Maker, for allowing me to be an important part of this tale of grand splendor and majesty. To witness all of this with the eyes you have given. To enjoy and revel in the majesty of your creation and the coming one. These you have given freely. Blessed am I to have a God-given soul and spirit unmatched in all of creation. And if I might be so presumptuous, I will also thank you for all of this, on behalf of all the others who are likewise so blessed.

And guide me in the way that I might best help bring to fruition your good and great designs. Thank you, especially that you hear me, and that you listen, and have set in motion all these wondrous things for me, you, and yours.

All these praises we sing in thy name - Amen!

INSPIRATION, PROPHECY AND RECKONING

On a few occasions, when writing about topics of a religious or spiritual nature, I have paused to ask myself in a rather cynical way,

"Do you think you are a prophet or something?"

Surely, I think not, for my mind is often neither here nor there; inconsistent and not commonly abiding in all that is good. I am just a person, reflecting upon my thoughts, refining them, and ideally expressing the best result in the best way that I can. Often the better of my realizations are born of my brokenness, and my struggles, and so even my many failings seem to have some purpose.

Nonetheless, at times, I *do feel* as though *some* of my thoughts arise within me *as if* from a higher source. At times, it *feels* as if I have tapped into some meaning that is beyond my own ordinary capacity. So, in this way, I *do* feel sometimes that the *better* among my ideals have been *inspired*, in a manner of speaking.

Is it *wrong* to feel inspired in some of our thoughts and expressions?

Don't many of us feel this way from time to time?

Don't we all feel an inspired voice within us at one time or another?

Don't we all sometimes feel as if something beyond our own capability has arisen within, and perhaps for a good reason?

And if we all feel this way from time to time, is it *so offensive* that we should say so?

It seems that nowadays we are all very comfortable speaking from the most negative and basest of voices arising within us, but we are somehow embarrassed of speaking aloud in that higher and more inspired voice arising at times from within.

Doesn't that seem somewhat backward?

So, while I have *felt* inspired in writing most of the passages included here, I cannot claim with certainty that I am providing an infallible or accurate account of every topic, for I am but a simple man.

So, here is my answer:

If *any* particular words *seem* to be coming from God or *seem* to be inspired towards the greater good, then *you may*, if you wish, consider those words to be prophetic or inspired.

But if you, in your heart of hearts, do *not* feel that any particular words are from God and are *not* for the greater good, then you may likewise consider those same words to be non-prophetic, and you may then move kindly along – happily expressing your own ideas and beliefs.

Yet I urge you to please pause and reflect carefully upon *all* that you see and hear.

Perhaps there are some gems residing in some very plain soil.

So, please judge the value of *each* sentiment *individually* and most carefully *for yourself.*

And while sincere questioning is *always* in order, in no instance try to obstruct, persecute, obfuscate, or destroy these or any other intentionally enlightened sentiments or the messengers of those words.

For God may have allowed the *good* to be tormented and persecuted for the *greater* good in times past and, at times, to give complete allowance for ill-mindedness and brutishness to be overlooked. But now, not always will this be so.

For in due time, the long-suffering allowances in letting *all* offenses stand, fairly considering the outside chance that they might somehow be justified and thereby let stand, will be exhausted. In due time, that which is broken will be fixed, or if unfixable, merely discarded.

Ages have passed in *fair consideration* of all things. And in due time, either progressively or all at once, those fallacies, wrongs, evils, and their *related sufferings* will be sheared and cleaved away. The chaff *will*, in due time, be separated from the wheat.

I am by no means without sin, nor is anything, or anyone, but here is how it will be:

If a man (or any *thing*) has 10% blight, then that will be removed, leaving the good 90%. And a small hole shall be in that being, and the portion which is worthy of remaining shall do so.

And if another has 90% darkness and bane, be comforted, that 90% yoke of evil shall be cast away from him and forever lost. This, too, is good, for the 10% that remains is joyous and worthy of life.

And if somehow one part is 100% detrimental or evil, then that part will be 100% removed. While none of us is without *any* good, by this exaggerated example, this one would be removed fully; by grace, never reconstructed. Not forgotten, but not fondly remembered either.

Thus, time will refine and remove *from us* the miserable and horrific, through the effects of the yearning for good by the Greater Consciousness. Setbacks may occur, and there may appear to be an ebb and flow, but at some juncture, the result becomes inevitable; that which is neither good nor fitting will be removed or replaced within us collectively. The reverse of this is irrational and antithetical to the nature and direction of the Greater Consciousness, which constitutes the will of God.

In what variation of an ultimate Paradise could this be otherwise, that evil, pain, and suffering might continue to dwell within and around us?

So, an understanding of these words will help usher in a new era in which we experience Life in an expanded and elevated form.

And be careful in reprimanding one another – for that which is to be eradicated – the cause of suffering and woe – is within *each* of us. Rather, work to *be* good, and right, and joyous, and hopeful - lest you be left with mostly holes in your souls.

Fear not, for this is meant to be a great uplifting – the ultimate elimination of brokenness, sorrow, and suffering. And while this may or may not occur fully within our individual lifetimes, we are still a part of this ongoing process.

The time has come for us to collectively stop losing, and to magnify only the winning spirit of God within and without. Glorify the Sublime in his unmanifested and manifested forms. Honor all that he created, and in his spirit strive to rise above or eliminate all suffering and ignorance. Embolden and intentionally empower all that is good.

Of these things, I have felt deeply and highly inspired.

Sower of the New

I. Sower of the new, master architect and builder supreme, eternal thanks to you for this space, this moment, with I in it and all that this entails. Beyond dreams and mightier than fiction are your makings and designs, which have yielded this 'humble' moment of which I partake.

Blessed is the maker and the made and all that dwell in his house (his world, this world).

Blessed are we in this moment and the next, and more so if we are mindful of our inherent divinity. Especially blessed are we to observe and understand the magical essence of our very nature.

Blessed is our existence as we abide in each moment, and ever more heightened is our joy and power as we fully immerse with you in the reality of the now.

I will do my best to animate each moment,
this moment;
to live forwardly and boldly in the now.

II. Mighty is the magic of reality that binds each moment unto the next. Incredible, yes, even if I forget, or fail, or err in any way, the moments are still together stitched. The interconnectedness of reality persists and is strong beyond breaking, and is seemingly expansive beyond measure – despite my fleeting and shallow observance of its depth and majesty. Despite my doubts and questions, the orderly manner of reality carries on without fail.

The glue of the maker is strong and reliable, yielding a world that robustly and adaptively supports me and my kind. There is great stability compared against the absolute of chaos. All things tend to remain after days and nights pass. And on each morn, I can be assured of reality remaining intact. Despite my absent-minded thinking and dreaming, your world cradles me and awaits me upon each waking.

Thankful are we that this world is not fickle and breaking with each doubt, each fear, and not changing with each random thought. None of these affect your brilliant reality, yet from this safe nest we may have our random thoughts, doubts, and dreams.

Your world is never flinching, oh Lord. From this type of environment, and with the right mindset, a being could harbor great joy and accomplish great feats.

Live in me and through me, O' God, the Phenomenal One. But let me not forget that greater yet subtler part of you that binds all things and makes all things possible.

Fantastic in this moment,

Now and Always,

With Love,

Amen

Pitfalls Along the Pathway to Ultimate Victory

When the hounds of hell
	will seek you out.

And slate coldness
	grips your soul within.

Remember God has
	survived and ruled over
		all these things.

Every darkness he
	has endured for an eternity
		beyond our eternity.

Every pain and fear
	he has outlasted and overpowered.

And he will do so,
	again and again,
		for all time if needed.

And so you should now have the confidence in the knowledge that the good will persevere
> - and thereby effectuate the hastening of the ultimate good.

The undeniable truth is that the sooner we stop losing we shall win.

This is the certainty of the victory of that which is best
> - this is salvation - and the irreversible path of *Ultramation*.

This is,
> the beginning of the end,
>> of all the feeble creaks and moans
>>> of the beleaguered and afraid.

You, That Which Made Us, Are For Us

I ncredible and Ultimate One,

I cannot know, but at times, it seems that perhaps not everything is right with all things. And that observation is from my most honest and humble perceptions, of which you know the origin and state more than do I. If you are aware to that degree, then you know my innermost thoughts, and so it is pointless to conceal from you my thoughts and concerns. So, you know that I am comfortable with being honest and forthright in my thoughts and words.

I am sure that you like me for my honesty and directness, and I thank you for this atmosphere of openness.

Having arisen from and above the primordial chaos, I know that you are not fragile. You are strong and are not broken by our mere thoughts, doubts, or questions.

In this light of truthfulness and in the good faith of our friendship, I often question some of the notions that certain men have presented and forwarded concerning you:

Might you not be *all*-powerful? If so, might not *all* things be without trouble, sorrow, or pain?

Yet, do I not still admire and appreciate all of creation as an unfolding spectacular - grand beyond thoughts, words, and comparison?

Might you not be *all*-knowing? For such knowledge might preclude the encountering of any issues, travail, or woe.

Yet I am aware that your way of knowing must surpass, underlie, and supersede the manner of our more limited, conscribed, and focused form of thought. And I am assured that your knowledge is always directed toward an enhanced and better universe, which we might ultimately call paradise.

Might you not be *all*-good? Or else, could any evil or flawed thing exist or persist?

Yet I know that men do not define what is ultimately good, and that in our kinship with you, we share a bond within which our greater values, goals, and benefits are invariably shared. All that which is good has certainly been sought by you, and that which is good for you is certainly good for us, and that which is good for us is decidedly good for you. And that which we encounter as bane is likewise that which you encounter as bane. And all that is woe is becoming undone in your due time.

In my eyes, these three limitations explain more clearly the probable relationship between a conscious creator, all creation, and created consciousness. The resulting state is reflected by our current position, once upon a timeline within an inexplicable universe.

This reality is Your astounding awakening. It is a beautiful process of expansive unfolding in which we gladly partake. It is a task for which we are partly purposed, perhaps. And it is our awakening as well. God, you who have made us, are surely on our side, and we are inevitably on yours.

You, that which made us, are for us.

And I am for you.

Despite any limitation, any uncertainty, any error, any hardship,

We are for all that is for good.

Amen.

ONE WITH GOD

So, at this time, when you truly feel "at one with God," you suddenly realize that you no longer have any problem "submitting to God's will." For the ego stops all blind resistance upon recognizing that the God to whom you are submitting is *you*.

Albeit God is a far greater version of 'you', encompassing all others as well as all conceptual others. But *you* are a creation of God's – correction; a *part* of God's living universe. You are an extension or implementation of the Greater Consciousness. You are quite deeply and intrinsically a part of God.

As light emanates from its source, the two are considered inseparable; for he is as the sun as you are like a sunray.

Not two, but one; we share a form of consciousness with the Eternal One. Our awareness within this world is but borrowed from the sublime, and in that bond, we likewise share our most elemental values and goals.

So, now we can *truly* "Let go and let God," for God is, in fact, 'letting' us; He is empowering and hastening us in each moment.

Each of us still retains our own distinct individuality. Each of us, you and I, can now more truly *be* one with God. For we can now more clearly see that by failing to embrace the conscious element of Greater Consciousness within and without, we are only rejecting that greater and better part of ourselves.

In the past, perhaps in the context of some religious teachings, when being told to "submit to God," you might have wondered, "What is this invisible thing to whom I am supposed to submit?" And perhaps defiantly, some of us may have even felt, "I submit to *no one*."

But now, you are acknowledging that which is greater, stronger, and far more resilient, is that which also lives and breathes through you. Now, without resistance, you may soar into all you were meant to be. Being all that you can be – and nothing less.

God is the unmanifested everything, and everything is the manifestation of God. You are a discrete, focused, differentiated manifestation or emanation of the consciousness of God; a God that is of a conscious type which is more diffuse, broader, and greatly more generalized.

God is an underlying primordial force or consciousness of a type that we can't really know in our normal way of knowing, nor can we fully comprehend. A consciousness beyond our scope of consciousness. A being-ness that supersedes yet permeates being and substance.

An archetypal timeless source or matrix from which all things – including you – continuously arise and arose, both then, now, and always.

You *are* one with God, but one is the greater and one the lesser. Yet in some ways, the lesser is the greater, for God so very much 'wanted' to become manifest. God has endured all of eternity and so would suffer all for his creation, his manifestation, and his children. God thereby wanted to become, create, or become manifest *within* - and *as* - *all* things perpetually. While empowering all beings to exist individually, and to some extent encouraging them to become individuated and distinct; God wanted, at utmost, to become *you*.

And yes, from the inside looking out, from an existential viewpoint, *you* are God's utmost manifestation. You are His most favored child. And as a fully independent little piece of God, you have the faculties to think independently. Although we are only human, we are each endowed with capabilities and depth beyond what anyone can fully know or might typically express. So, each 'piece' can be so much more; every embodied emanation could be so much brighter. Truly, each of us could so greatly exceed our own normal mundane expectations and the seemingly binding expectations of our societies, contemporaries, and peers.

While overall this is a very heightened realization, it is a realization that can also be tinged with a hint of sadness. There is regret for all those occasions when we have forgotten or neglected this observation that we and our fellow man are one with God. We are somewhat tainted when we do not forever and always rise fully empowered by it.

Some would even go so far as to say that our failure to *be* consistently 'one with God' is a 'sin', and perhaps even a very fundamental form of sin. Perhaps it can be seen as a core type of human failing; a common form of 'under-performance' that, in turn, leads to many of our other problems and sins.

While we should always attempt to rise to the highest of our ideals, perhaps we need to detoxify and 'dial back' that overpowerful word 'sin' - just a little.

MISSING THE MARK

I believe that it is always important to put everything into proper perspective. It seems our ideas concerning 'sin' have become rather exaggerated and often excessively condemnatory, so perhaps this topic needs a little attention.

'Sin' is literally translated as 'missing the mark'. That was the very simple original meaning. In the practice of marksmanship, traditionally archery, it is seen as an error or a mistake when a skilled archer fails to hit the 'bull's eye'. Early philosophers and religious teachers always had to contend with the notion of imperfection, error, and tragedy within the world. After all, why did those failings exist at all? The notion of 'sin' does not necessarily *answer* many of these questions, nor does it adequately explain *why* these flaws exist; it is just a term that conveniently labels and acknowledges the inherent imperfections.

The notion of sin, although originally quite simple, has taken on many layers of moralistic overtones, such that it is now most often associated with various types of immorality, which typically occur by the 'breaking' of various codified rules of conduct. While those types of failings might certainly be included under the broad umbrella of sin, a true 'sin' is much simpler and more commonplace. It is any time we fail, any time anything fails, any time we have a valid expectation that is not met, and any time there is a valid goal that is not achieved.

In this context, each of us probably 'sins' many times a day. All day, every day, we fail in a hundred small ways. But of course, there are failures that are small and do not matter so much, and others that are much 'larger' and clearly more significant.

A perfectionist would insist pedantically that any 'sin', any failing, invalidates or ruins the entire system. But the universe, the ever-living creation of the Maker, while not perfect, is *never* invalidated.

Sin was not meant to be seen as some tragic inescapable flaw, but rather as the sum of the millions of simple imperfect occurrences, both large and small, that occur all along the way in this grand endeavor known as Life. Imperfections and failings would naturally occur when bringing an entire universe from a state of chaos into a more idealized state. Anyone who claims that *any* instance of a lack of perfection *entirely* invalidates any system is saying that *everything* is permanently broken from day one. That belief and manner of thinking are themselves *seriously flawed.*

Sin, in a more relevant sense, must include some type of harm done to another person, to oneself, to God, or to Life itself; otherwise, the error has very little or no significance. For something to matter, it has to matter.

Any sin or flaw can only be seen in the context within which it occurred, and certainly, some errors or flaws have a much more significant effect than others. Most of the errors and mistakes we make on a daily basis are literally of no noticeable effect.

While sin is actually any imperfection, error, or flaw, when viewed more dramatically, the more serious flaws, errors, and mistakes can indeed lead to pain, suffering, conflict, malady, and tragedy. And *that* is when they begin to matter significantly. That is when they become much more significantly 'wrong'.

When problems or failings occur, we attempt to correct them. We don't cry out in wails of defeatism and damnation. And *before* problems occur, we attempt to anticipate and avoid them. We best accomplish this, although this process is also laden with many failings, when we attempt to live and act in ways that will exemplify our greatest and highest nature.

Thus, sin is an unwanted but natural part of the universe in its unfolding. Sin also represents that which we wish to rise above; the problems, woes, and maladies which detract from Life. But the mere presence of sin does not negate the magnificence, beauty, or goodness of all that is or all that will be.

So let us not abandon *all* due to our many failings, errors, pains, and woes. Damnation or the judgment over all of creation is not ours to give. We must, in good faith, do *all* that we can to foster and enhance *all* of God's Creation, with the intention and hope that everything that is now broken will ultimately be fixed.

Sin (the very capacity for failing and error) clearly existed before us. We must conclude that it originated somehow within God or within the manifestation that occurred before us. Yet *that* sin, the very capacity for sin, and *all* sins, are and must be forgiven. These are but diversions or errors that will be corrected and improved as Greater Consciousness moves forward through time toward an ultimate destination.

For even now, in this imperfect era, we are one with God. God is with us, God is within us, and as God is fundamentally good, so are we *fundamentally* good. With a greater degree of certainty and dismissing definitions of 'good' versus 'bad,' concerning God and ourselves;

We are on the same side.

The 'sin' or imperfection within us or outside us is our common enemy. The gradual or immediate resolution of all transgressions, sorrows, and tragedies is our personal and common goal (a goal shared by Greater Consciousness). The overall situation may improve in our individual lifetimes, or not; but bear in mind that a form of salvation may occur in an instant. Change, normally gradual, *can* make astonishing leaps, and even more astounding paradigm shifts can occur at certain key junctures.

But even if it takes an arduous eternity, we (God and God within us) will continue to progress and prevail over all manner of maladies and evils.

This is the only way.

From this perspective, sin and all associated flaws are forever overcome and forgiven.

With this perspective, we can better understand our cohesion, our oneness with God; the source of all things, and the source of triumph being realized over all that is broken.

The Only Way to Fly

So, when we referred earlier to submitting to God's will, it does not mean that we must submit to any specific religious teaching or any questionable or dubious notion of God. Nor do we mean submitting *blindly* to any priests, prophets, or teachers – nor to any of their impassioned or sometimes coercive teachings, unless their reasoning and merits are sound.

Additionally, we do not expect immediate 'perfection' or absolute freedom from 'sin' and failure, even when we are trying our best to be "in tune" with God or "one with God".

We are simply attempting to draw ourselves closer to, and become more aware of, that underlying and overarching form of Consciousness, which is far greater than we are. In that which comprises the greater and better part of us, therein we will find a small semblance of the Living God.

In striving to become more attuned, we wish only to love more deeply and appreciate more fully the

Almighty and Everlasting One and the entirety of his creation. Thereby, our actions in this world may become more harmonious and appropriate under many circumstances.

And if this *still* remains unclear, one might ask,

"So then, what is this *god* to whom I am submitting?"

Recognize that on some level, that you *are* already one with God. Your spirit or consciousness is made in the image of His. You consist (in the state of your pure awareness) of the same basic essence or fabric as does He – albeit of a different form and construct.

Despite these commonalities, you exist as an individual, so a literal 'one-ness' is not what is implied here.

However, even though you are an individual, you share an inner *facet* of consciousness – a metaphysical connection. Via this connection, within the depths of awareness, a greater understanding of that which cannot be understood may be better *approximated*.

But while it is difficult (beyond impossible) to *fully know* God in this manner, it is much simpler (and as intended) to more fully *experience this natural connection* with God, and thereby best experience this world into which you are purposefully embodied. To this end, and in this way, we may more fully come to love and appreciate the Loving and Living God.

So, it is this *connection* that we might best *experience*, not an absolute understanding – for that is beyond all possibility to us in this world.

One way to envision this is to imagine that you are always 'flying' through Life - soaring in this life in tandem with the greater unmanifested God. You in this world, and He in the other – yet both of you together.

He has manifested within you the ability to fully act in this world. So, you may pilot by yourself - or *you* may pilot and with *him* navigating.

To 'fly' in this way requires some openness and sensitivity, but when accomplished - and when in process - it *can* feel *so* right. It makes for an awesomely fun flight!

Your experience becomes clear and strong – at times, this can be unmistakable.

You will feel calm, confident, and empowered, without distraction or fear.

You *will know* that this is the way to fly.

This is the only way to fly.

OF WHICH WAYS,
WHO AND WHAT?

I. You are the subtle underlying all things.
The moment that lies in wait already ahead of
       – yet before – this moment.

You are the future that unspins the past.
Ever present, always changing,
yet unchanged in the now.

Mystery beyond mystery,
Wonder beyond mere awe.
You are forgotten, unseen,
yet the foundation of all certitude
      - both real and opined.

Originator and sustainer of all that is physical,
and of bright consciousness,
and all things both real and unreal.

Hard like rock, yet subtle like spirit,
you move amidst all things with bold stealth.

You are the essence of all things,
The being within all beings.
The thought within all thoughts,
And the act of thinking that binds and apprehends all thought.

You are the soul within all souls,
and the feeling source of all feelings.
You are the origin and pattern of shape and form,
and you are the mighty stuff of matter; expansive and heavy.

You are the action that yields all actions,
The energy that fuels all reaction.
The energy that is the hard stuff of matter.
The energy that is the ethereal art of mind and spirit.

You flow like a river amongst and amidst all things.
Forming, bonding, shifting, changing -
Always coalescing into something new.

Something, sometimes, yet more amazing always arising;
On each day, a new miracle is born.
And then on some days – as we thank you -
a new miracle far greater and grander in scale
ascendantly occurs.

And these miracles burst forth from time immemorial
Into the infinity of tomorrows.
And in every sense that may be considered real,
And even when no change occurs in the physical,
the smallest shift of my mind-stuff, my perception,
can reframe all that is, so that it is again new and bold.

A whole new reality and existence can be born
in the simplest shift of my mind.
And what more can shift
in the massed awareness of beings
- that can certainly amount to a new -
and yes – ever better reality?

II. Yet to me, despite all of these incomprehensible attributes and aspects, You are seemingly like a person, a personality, perhaps even with form. Is this but a weakness of my earth-bound state of mind? Can I only imagine an advanced ethereal entity in human form?

For certainly, you are all forms, and so could have any form. Yet you are beyond form as we know it. Apprised to all forms, can we not conceive you betrothed to but one?

And of personality, I imagine you to be kind and wise. For what maker would despise all his creation?

But I must fathom that your personality bestows and bears *all* traits, and is at the core of all personalities. Yet you are beyond personality. So, I recognize that your personality is of a type that is beyond my realm of possible experience, and therefore, I may only conceive it in my own partial or fragmented manner.

Also, I perceive you as having a voice that is directly concerned with me and my affairs. For I am you - in some measure - and you are within me and all around me. Intertwined and interwoven, we are one, yet distinct, and I have no shame - but rather great pride - in acknowledging or affirming this.

Accompanying one another always, we are the best of friends.

Love embodying and superseding all love, I know that Your love for me is immeasurable. And You know that I, existing in this physical and human world, remain true in my love and devotion to you and the entirety of your creation - both seen and unseen.

While subject to the exigencies and turmoils of this world, I am nonetheless a steadfast lover, protector, and protagonist of your creation. As an agent on your behalf, you empower me to this end. In this, I am grateful that you, the Almighty, have made me to be always happy and healthy, and to live forever in the worlds of form and the formless. For you have set this into effect in the moments before the time that is just now.

For all these things, and the wondrous relationship that unfolds anew with each dawn, I am truly a grateful and joyous participant and partner.

In best remembrance,

Always and forever,

Amen

THINGS THAT MATTER

From a more practical perspective, it might be of considerable value to reflect upon those things which matter the most in our day-to-day lives. Basically, it would be useful to understand which things matter the most, so that we might better know where and how to spend our limited time in this world. While 'that which matters' may vary somewhat from person to person, and may fluctuate even within an individual person's lifespan (from one season to another), the following are subjects that will have general value for *all* people, in *all* seasons.

Whether or not one agrees that the following represent validly 'important' concepts, it would be advisable for each of us to independently reflect upon, evaluate, and define what *is* truly important to ourselves - and why.

Can we not simply sit and think about what is important and meaningful to us, so that we may direct ourselves in those ways?

Or else, we may be just billowing and blustering blindly against the futile winds of randomness.

Things that do matter:

Life, Love, Health, Joy, Character, Truth, and Faith.

Not necessarily in that order.

For starters, let's set aside any textbook 'cut and dried' definitions or biased personal preconceptions regarding these characteristics or values.

Each of these qualities, in reality, covers a wide range of variation, color, and depth. An entire set of books would need to be written in order to adequately address the scope and dimensionality of *each* of these topics. We will suffice with a few paragraphs for each, relying instead upon innate wisdom (or 'common sense') within each individual to appropriately flesh out the details.

It is hoped that despite a rather simplistic summary, we can begin to 'step outside the box' regarding our potentially jaded perceptions concerning these seven, perhaps over-referenced, virtues or qualities.

Of course, there are many additional 'things that matter', such as companionship, sleep, or sheer luck. Also, there are some fundamental physical resources that *really* matter a great deal, like food, water, shelter, energy, oxygen, etc.

The themes presented here were not intended to be all-inclusive, but instead, they present a series of inspired or carefully considered thoughts regarding seven vital qualities. These passages occurred to me at the time of my mother's waning health and just before her passing.

Before reflecting upon the topics concerning things that truly matter, let's first take a look at some contrasting ideas regarding things that *do not* matter.

Things that do not matter;

Normalcy – doing, being, or saying anything just to 'fit in'.

Mundane or superfluous details - unless they bring us some joy or peace.

Not a very big list, really, even though at times we may negatively wish to feel like "nothing matters." Sometimes it just seems *easier* that way. Perhaps we feel that if "nothing matters," we won't have to worry or be concerned. If nothing matters, we can just 'let go'.

But that is not reality.

And if "easy" is our main concern, we could just as easily "let go" and flow with the notion that some things *do* matter.

Actually, *all* things, or anything, may matter at one time or another. But some things don't merely "matter" in our typical way of perceiving the word, for they are pivotal or overarching in their importance. Some things have an almost ultra-importance, and we can thereby say that they are "supra-relevant."

All things that are not directly evil, destructive, or vile are, in fact, wondrous and magical.

> ***That which surpasses the darkness is the light, which is to be cherished and emphasized.***

That which is undesirable is destined to be de-emphasized, phased out, or extincted in the ultimate timeline of the universe. Within our own minds, a microcosm of this process exists; that which matters, and which is good or worthwhile, replaces that which does not matter. That which does not pass muster or is directly undesirable naturally fades. The 'lesser' is often nearly extinguished or fully replaced successively by that which is 'better'.

Is it not logical that consciousness will gradually emphasize, evolve, and tend toward that which is good and desirable, and will accordingly eclipse, eliminate, or rectify all that is broken, vile, or bane?

But in the here and now, at times, we must "let go" and not "care too much". This may seem contradictory, but not everything in life is straightforward or one-dimensional.

There is a delicate balance between caring too much and not enough.

But is this balance really so difficult?

In any case, for the greater part of bearing and direction, we would best tend towards those things that matter.

Without the values that really matter
 our lives become broken, tired, and even futile.
  Sadness, emptiness, frustration, and anxiety creep in.
   So, should we not nurture those qualities which matter the most?
    And perhaps become distracted less often
     by lesser musings and hollow pursuits?
      And more clearly so, should we not divert almost entirely
       from negative and blighted thought forms and pursuits?

So, perhaps this all seems far too simple. And if one should need more detail, it is surely forthcoming. But, if the preceding is all you need to be set upon your true and best course, then why tarry upon the tedium of additional details?

Nonetheless, we shall proceed with a glance into each of the things which strongly matter;

Life, Love, Health, Joy, Character, Truth, and Faith.

LIFE

Life, so clearly, matters. How precious it is.
Even those of us who believe in a timeless hereafter,
or of a perpetual nature to our life's essence, still
cling dearly to *this* life.

Even in times of great despair, do not forsake
the precious time of *this* life;

for though the time beyond appears infinite,
the time of *this* life, by comparison, is so
fleeting.

Yet Life itself is something greater.
The life force that fills us is divine and sublime.
Primordial yet ever renewing – the Life that fills us
fills the universe with all forms of consciousness.
Conscious beings are connected to God
- the Source - via their innermost being(s).
And thereby, all lives are intertwined
and shared.

So how do I focus upon, or enhance the value of Life?
By honoring it, by thinking and reflecting upon
how it is a magical gift, beyond one's own
accomplishment.

By appreciating and focusing on the good in Life.
By not cheapening, diminishing, or spoiling it.
By not diminishing the value of Life in
yourself, others or God – the life force
that fills all beings.

Now some might ask, "But what if I still don't know what force it is that animates me?"

If you do not kindly know yourself or that Greater Consciousness…

If uncertainty exists concerning what this *life* really is…

If you can't find an appreciation of how Life is a magical inner connection to a greater, deeper consciousness…

Then perhaps consider a simple and relaxing practice of inner discovery. Any approach that broadens the understanding and *acceptance* of the self (or the soul) is worthwhile. For example, meditation, mindfulness, honest prayers from the heart, or any similar reflective practice, can help us gain an understanding of this inner being *directly*. For these are exercises *of* the being, rather than attempts to think *about* the nature of being or to simply objectify it.

While we are all children of God, some seem to be more enlightened than others. Many of those enlightened teachers implore us primarily to ensure that our hearts are right with God (the Son of Man), or similarly, that we should become more 'in harmony' with Life (the Buddha). These concepts may have been predated by the Vedic teachings of 'right understanding' (Krishna). All of these teachings imply that we can be more or less in harmony with Life and the Greater Consciousness, which is at its source.

The very idea that we can be either 'in sync' or 'out of sync' with ourselves, with Life, or with a Greater Consciousness is clearly worth *some degree* of reflection. If some of history's greatest spiritual teachers acknowledge this potential for "disconnectedness", then perhaps we too should consider bringing ourselves into accord with Life, and thereby with The Ultimate.

And how do we do that if we truly know neither our innermost selves nor the potential nature of the spirit of God, which lies just beyond?

And that is a rhetorical question, in case it was not clear.

Perhaps consider the advice and methods of self-reflection as espoused by enlightened holy men throughout time. Or simply engage in *any* sincere and hopeful act of self-reflection, under any terms and conditions that you deem appropriate. Perhaps in doing so, we can more clearly come to understand our own lives and *what we are* fundamentally. Perhaps we can strengthen our bonds and connections to a Greater Consciousness.

Beyond these and many other deliberate techniques for self-discovery, the basic, ordinary awareness of Life may be said to be quite apparent.

The awareness of Life is available to all the living.

Even in its most basic form, and without any 'enlightened higher understanding' and without any formal 'teaching', ordinary Life is astonishingly extraordinary.

Life is worthy in and of its own accord.

In the *simplest* embodiment of its ever-so-elaborate nature;

the purpose of Life is to live.

And in that light, must we ever so painstakingly define, dissect, and attempt to intellectually justify each thing which is so clearly evident?

Life matters. (And that is a period at the end of the last sentence.)

And is it not ever so clear, without further elaboration, that Life, above all, is sacred?

Hence, fortunately, an entire book need not be written on the topic.

LOVE

ove, what of Love? Could we, or more importantly, *should* we exist without it? That is not to say that we should cease to exist for lack thereof, but rather, by all means, seek to find and nurture it within our hearts.

For I know that Love is real, so why should it be denied my heart?

It is Love that binds us to one another and endears us to the sheer reality that is God's creation. Do not pretend that you do not know what Love is. So, *focus* your being on Love and not hate.

As the Good Shepherd, child of God, explained, this is the highest commandment;
　　To love God above all, with all our heart and being.
　　　And to love one another just as we love ourselves.
　　　　This *implies* at its very foundation that we love ourselves first…
　　　　Not *most*, but first or fundamentally.

Most notably, the prominent keyword throughout this passage is 'love'.

The greatest commandment consists essentially of Love.

Love that inner Life force within yourself, which is your connection to God and one another. And love also this physical being into which you are made.

Furthermore, to love God, a love that might seem abstract, should we not also love all creation – the very manifestation of God?

None of us is perfect, but God has breathed the precious magic of Life into each of us. When we are not mindful of this, we may treat ourselves, or one another, too harshly. That is not love. Remember to remember that each person is but a child. More than that, a child of God.

Treat them and yourselves as tenderly as you would treat a child, for hate wilts not only its object but also its wielder.

Hate decays the hater's soul and cripples his sense of well-being.

Is it not clear that one should dwell upon Love, for hate cannot abide at the same time in the same heart with Love? Which would you choose to fill your heart: the dark, dismal rot of hate, or the bright and joyous light of Love?

To the extent that you *can* choose, do so wisely.

You know this to be true, correct, and wise. This is proper and healthy. It is good for you and those around you. If you are gripped by hate, remember that hate is the death of the soul in the now. So, shake it off. Break it off. Again and again, if necessary.

Shake it off as often as it arises and replace it with Love. No one but you can control your heart, so do not say "I can't" or "I won't." Do not cloak yourself in helpless pity.

To be a lover of Life, you will and you must. So just do it!

Remember that Love comes in many forms and none of them are wrong. Love for a man of a woman, and of a woman for a man, are powerful forms of Love. Let not that specialized form of love turn into possessiveness or other forms of hate.

The Love of a parent for a child is similarly uniquely strong. It reflects the way that God loves all of his creation. In a circular way, our love for God can be shown through our love of all that he has created – his children endowed with his awareness especially.

He who loves all of God's creation surely loves God, and he who loves above all the innermost Life-force loves God in the highest. The Life-force within is what allows you to perceive and appreciate all things. Your consciousness is *holy* and is, in some ways, a direct connection to God, and in other ways, it is, in fact, a small piece of God. You are an embodiment consisting of energy emanating from, and thus partly comprising, the Greater Consciousness. Cradle and adore this precious light of Life – within and without.

Love your innermost being, all others, and the universe, which is the creation of God. Love the greater consciousness that is God – which created all and permeates all with sustaining Life-force in every moment.

Nurture this wondrous force of Life with Love.

> ***Life is like a flame, and it is fueled by our Love for the living universe.***

HEALTH

And some will surely ask, "What about health? If we are such spiritual beings, why is my physical body of any importance?"

As stated before, Life, - this life, in *this* embodiment - is a very precious gift. You *are* in the here and now; incarnate in the flesh *for a reason*. Perhaps it is a reason beyond reason. And even if not for a reason, then what difference does it make? Who needs a reason?

We are *here*, alive in *this* flesh, but for a moment in the infinity of time. And *this* time on *this* earth is golden, whatever your condition.

So, while you should honor Life with Love and connect in a deeper understanding with your inner Life-force – your immortal soul - you should also treat the health of your physical human body in this world as if it were more precious than gold. Value it, nourish it, protect it.

When you are unhealthy in any way, you will experience pain, and this will cloud your ability to love and enjoy the symphony that is your inner consciousness in joyous harmony with this world. This interplay of the world of consciousness dancing and intermingling with the world of matter occurs largely via your very physical body.

Eat well, avoid what is unhealthy, stay fit, and exercise.

Is this so absurdly difficult in some way?

Do not indulge in harmful excess or attend unwarranted hazards. Seek the advice of the scientist and the physician to ensure that you are not only long-lived but also that your days may be filled with a healthy form of happiness.

For happiness arises more naturally from a state of good health. In good health, happiness more naturally resides. For it is difficult, though not impossible, to fully experience happiness and joy when we are experiencing pain or physical malady.

So, is it not plainly straightforward that one should nourish his or her own physical health? Would we not call someone "foolish" who would choose to do otherwise?

Being aware of how we treat our bodies, we can observe the maxim of 'everything in moderation' to help guide us if the clarity of obviousness is lacking.

And if there is still some uncertainty about what is best, we can reach out to those who study good health for more detailed advice.

In any case, apply a simple measure of *awareness and effort* to the topic of health.

Act as if good health really matters – because it really does.

It is a fundamental underpinning to enjoying and loving *this* life in *this* world.

JOY

Now, if you value and nurture an appreciation of all the aforementioned (Life, Love, and Health), you will most likely find joy quite naturally.

In addition to experiencing the joy that naturally arises from a right mindset, also *directly* seek out, seek to understand, and seek to focus on *joy*. Discover what it is, where it comes from, and from whence it arises – and above all, *enjoy*.

Ours is both an inward and an outward journey. If there is an activity that brings you joy directly or indirectly, pursue it. Any joy that brings harm to no one simply adds great value to this life. Do not waste your time on empty or dry pursuits... unless they somehow bring about joy.

If there is a place that always brings you joy, go to that place often.

I am not speaking in riddles here, just follow your joy and it will lead you to the activities, pursuits, people, and places that give you true happiness. There you will find your place in this world. But there, one may more easily find an *inner* path to joy as well.

But what is joy? Must we ask? Perhaps some of us need to reflect or work inwardly on how we can experience or find joy. Are there things that should give us joy, but which we have failed to appreciate? What is joy, and why should it be missing? When joy is missing, we cannot *always* assume that it will be found *externally*. Although at times, seemingly, it can.

Joy can be a characteristic of being that one can solely amplify to a large extent. Yet joy, in this life, is most often the merging of a joyous inner nature with the object of that joy. It is intended, by nature, that we enjoy a joyous bond to this world – within which we abide, which we have been given.

Joy can be found in the harmony of a pursuit that fully resonates with the pursuer. Joy is magnified in an activity that engages the healthy inner Life-force and a healthy body together - acting upon the God-given resources, events, and entities of this world.

Is this all so unclear? Could it not be simpler to say, "Just pursue joy"?

Follow that which makes you smile, and when following any path, remember to smile often despite the many bumps in the road.

If joy seems to be waning, perhaps practice *allowing* yourself to be more able to simply enjoy that which *is*.

Perhaps we have failed to fully accentuate appreciation and that proverbial 'attitude of gratitude'.

Directly pursue the activities and follow the pursuits that bring you joy, but also remain open to appreciating and enjoying *whatever* life may bring.

Overall, regarding your pursuits, assume that the resonance between you and what attracts you is there by an act of the Maker. The joys you find in your pursuits in this world are perfectly natural and normal. The sense of harmony you find within these pursuits need not be the same for each person. There is no standard of normalcy in these matters; our differentiation and diversity of tastes, interests, and capabilities are there by the designs of God via nature. The full expression of our passions and curiosities is of great and inspiring collective value; the varied accomplishments of mankind are a testimony to this.

So, instead of seeking to hide behind normalcy, follow your *own* joy as you would follow a guide through the wilderness.

For those who have a strong and true passion, they are surely blessed.

Thus, your Joy in following your own healthy pursuits will lead you to the Love of Life.

Your Love of Life will be your reward for coming in tune with and following your innate sense of Joy.

CHARACTER

Character is important primarily because we do not exist alone but rather in societies with other human beings who can contribute to – or detract from – our experience of this reality in enormous ways. All of us, together, are children of God – descendants and siblings having the same essential nature. We must, therefore, actively strive toward the higher of our ideals regarding how we treat others. This is no matter in which to be careless, callous, or overly capricious.

Character is to your social existence as health is to your physical existence. You must exhibit some degree of fair, respectful, and proper behavior towards others, or else your life will be filled with mishaps and calamities at the hands of man.

While some are persecuted or harassed *unfairly*, if you have a glaring lack of character, you will naturally be ostracized or punished for your offending behaviors and attitudes. In contrast, a strong character wards off the bullying of lesser brutes and their weak-minded minions.

Having character will mean having some *principles* regarding your conduct towards others. These principles dictate that, at best, you will try to treat them as they wish to be treated. More fundamentally, it is important that we not *mistreat* one another. That we will treat others with kindness and fairness is the ideal, but to *do no harm* is the mere baseline.

As a simple guide, treat other individuals kindly as you would treat a childlike version of yourself, but also give them the respect deserved by an adult.

In your activities, pursuits, and words, avoid harming others as much as possible. Be strong in your own ideals and conduct yourself accordingly, yet, be forgiving to others when they fail to do so. This builds character, and character garners respect. Mutual and reciprocal expressions of character have the effect of forging connectivity and a sense of belonging and camaraderie.

When viewed in this light, Character is like the main building block of our civilization. Through character, we can work together to build great things and embark upon great journeys collectively. Without it, the bonds of mutual trust and cohesiveness that hold our society together are disintegrated. None of our collective achievements can be possible without some measure of character.

With bonds carefully fostered and enabled by character, together, we can share in the enjoyment of events – great and small. All the great wonders of mankind – the great structures, technologies, and the arts – are made possible by individuals with great yet humble character. They are, at best, working and playing well together, fostering common joy through the love of one another as children of a wondrous God.

The Life-force that animates us *demands* that we treat each other with respect, care, and dignity.

Developing character can seem difficult at times, but in fact, it is rather easy. It is much easier to build character than to wallow in selfish disregard for those we encounter.

Difficult?

It is the *lack* of character that will prove to be a much greater difficulty – a burdensome limitation upon one's own prospects in life.

Begin to see your fellow man not as your detractor, but as your cohort, your companion, your comrade, and your friend.

Share life's joy with one another while you still can.

TRUTH

Truth is important, quite obviously, or else we will all be stumbling blindly in the darkness.

Without Truth, there is only the brokenness of confusion.

The success of the human species resides largely in our capacity to discern the truth concerning any matter at hand. Our natural (or God-given) curiosity inspires us to discover how things work, to deduce what *causes* events, and to discard false premises. These are all *forms* of the pursuit of truth, of which there are many more.

Our ancestors believed that disease was caused by gremlins and spirits, but now we know it is often from bacteria and viruses. It was important for man to seek the truth, and now we can effectively cure or prevent many diseases due to our increased understanding of the *truth*. We can also avoid irrational behaviors that might have involved false 'cures' that often may have exacerbated rather than relieved the condition. When observing some of the rites of medicine from ages past, we can clearly see that, very often, the cure was worse than the disease.

In many ways, man can be seen as evolving from the darkness of ignorance progressively into the light of understanding.

This is Truth; knowing what is real from what is illusion, conjecture, and fantasy.

Some would think that science is not the way of God.

Do you believe darkness and ignorance are the ways of God?

What kind of God is that?

Untruth.

That which benefits Life is good. The truth regarding any matter will allow Life to benefit rather than being perpetually bound to any related problems in ignorance.

The human spirit is such that it will advance against pain, suffering, and all forms of problems. However, it often does so by availing itself of the Truth, at the expense of discarded falsehoods and misconceptions.

Is this not a good thing?

> ***To sharpen our understanding of truth***
> ***often involves the discarding of false premises***
> ***and conclusions.***

To pursue Truth and thereby solve problems through understanding is indeed a noble cause. To eliminate suffering and enhance the civilization of your fellow man – this is a most worthwhile pursuit.

And the pursuit of Truth can involve an inner pathway as well; ensuring that one's core beliefs (as much as possible) reflect the Truth and are not in conflict with any of Life's greater truths.

If you are fortunate enough to live in a world of creature comforts, yet find yourself uncomfortable, one might suspect that you are experiencing some inner conflict with Truth. You may have identified with a set of ideas that are inharmonious with the Truth, leading to a sense of conflict or inner turmoil.

Now, at times, those who are more advanced and have intentionally aligned themselves with some perspective of Truth have been sometimes persecuted by those who are ignorant, confused, and brutish. Notwithstanding, it is best if one can bring oneself in accord with the Truth, and through character, example, and patience allow others to gradually come into accord as well.

But let's not lose an important concept in complexity or diversion; in the absence of external pain or coercion, an inner conflict may indicate an unacknowledged or undiscovered truth. This conflict may resolve if one focuses on knowing and finding the Truth (either generally or concerning the specific matter toward which inner conflict exists).

A truth that is relevant yet missing will trouble you in the same way that an empty belly signals the pangs of hunger. When the truth you seek is finally found or understood, it will be a momentous event for you. A tremendous relief and a significant 'leveling up' will occur. A roadblock along your life's pathway will be removed, along with the accompanying conflict.

In some cases, understanding a specific truth is an important milestone in one's individual development, even though many others may have already acquired that particular element of understanding. There is no shame in this; it does not diminish the truth or its significance *to you* in your own personal journey. You do not have to be the first person to realize something for it to be meaningful. And certainly, there are some other truths that you might have perceived more clearly and much sooner than most of your peers. So do not let the fear of embarrassment cause you to cling to falsehood or become pugnaciously entrenched in any particular notion.

Learning and growing can seem challenging at times because we all tend to become heavily invested in our 'beliefs' which we assume to be true. Often, in searching for truth, we discard only what opposes our entrenched beliefs and hold on to only that which resonates. It can seem extremely difficult, after surrounding ourselves for years in familiar echo chambers filtering into a type of tunnel vision, to divest oneself of a misaligned belief or 'untruth' – even if valid evidence to the contrary is observed. But when we step beyond a paradigm that is untrue, into one that is *more* true, the shift is generally for the better. Such a shift (letting go of deeply rooted falsehoods or biases) can be monumentally positive – yet often initially accompanied by some uncomfortable growing pains. Thus, concerning the acquisition of truth (or the shedding of misnomer), just as with the exercise of physical muscle, it can be said: no pain, no gain.

In some rare cases, you may, through diligence and perseverance, realize or discover a truth that no one in our civilization has yet understood or documented. By revealing such knowledge, or Truth, you will provide great benefit and advancement to your beloved fellow beings. And often these truths will further unlock vast, auspicious new seas of knowledge and awareness.

Those who pursue knowledge, especially Truth, whether inwardly or outwardly, are therefore properly exalted by God and mankind alike.

FAITH

Lastly, we should focus on Faith. Although perhaps it is Faith which should be foremost, as it is the foundation of all the others. Life, and all virtues, and all that is good, are ultimately based on, and arise from, Faith. When all other qualities seem fragile, lost, or weak, faith alone can sustain us.

This does not necessarily mean having faith in any specific thing or any specific belief, but rather a faith in *all* things. For the sum of all things is the domain of the underlying Almighty.

This type of faith is the faith in all that is beyond you, the faith in the infinite unknown. It is in this faith that we fundamentally and ultimately reside.

Some say by faith and by grace do we exist in the afterlife. But more importantly, by faith and grace, we also exist in *this* life. In the present moment, we are animated by a means beyond ourselves and beyond our own efforts. And so we perpetually reside in this existence solely via faith and grace.

Your Life does not persist moment by moment due to any of your own devices or efforts. All that you are, and the very moment in which you now subsist, are manifested, surrounded, and supported by the great beyond – the infinities of time, space, and consciousness. Nothing that you do causes *you* to exist in this moment, and to the extent that you do, it is granted or given – in each moment - by all that is greater than us.

> **There, in the moment of our own undoing, we find Faith, and God.**

Faith is the opposite of fear, and when faced with the absolute uncertainty within which we exist, the absolute certainty of our existence becomes a matter of faith.

In the vast expanse of the conscious void, where chaos defines everything as but sameness and difference, we find that all which is good and wonderful arose from this chaos through a conscious act of primal *faith*.

Faith is the primordial sustaining force, and it rose up from the void as the good and vital consciousness of Life.

Faith is the essential component of consciousness that allowed God to exist. God first had faith – and this is the fundamental volition that said, in words beyond words, that despite all the reasons *not* to be, "I am!"

So, when faced with any personal fear over things, physical or psychological, realize that God, in his greater form of consciousness, will hold all things together. The Almighty, who has endured all things and has still sustained all of creation, will not fail in *this* simple moment, nor the next.

In our most difficult times, we may need to shed all other attachments, thus faith can sometimes appear to be at odds with everything else.

This may be the hardest for us to grasp, but Faith is like a threshold or a bottom line of sorts, below which nothing will pass. All else may fade away just as our physical body does in death. But in Faith, we recognize that fear need not exist. Fear and anxiety will not coexist with Faith, although we might need to find Faith on the other side of our fears.

If this seems esoteric or enigmatic, it may be best to visualize God as all-powerful, and then we may reside in the knowledge that whatever occurs is somehow "meant to be" and for the greater good of all.

Via Faith alone might we attest to an afterlife, for we do not, in all sincerity, *know* what exists 'on the other side'. Only by Faith do I expect my discrete and individual soul to carry on. Just as we abide in Faith, day by day, that God in his grace will provide for and allow the conscious soul to exist moment by moment in *this* world, so we have Faith that he solely may grant us some form of life in the next. This is as he in his greater form of consciousness, sees fit.

As such, a belief in an afterlife is *purely* a matter of Faith, since we do not have direct knowledge of these affairs. So, in Faith, we entrust the just disposition or continuation of our discrete souls, or any portions thereof, to the grace of the Ultimate (the Redeemer). In Faith, we have a firm resolution that the arrangement regarding this and all matters will be appropriate and for the Greater Good. This is Faith in its purest sense.

Yet Faith does not matter only in desperate times or when concerning overly serious matters. On *each day*, it is best to focus on our faith in all that is good. A key element of Faith resides in knowing that everything that is good is *greater* than all the problems and challenges which arise – even though sometimes the problems seem overly daunting and beyond our control.

Perhaps stating this in its opposite is more accurate; place faith in all that is beyond our control, knowing that all things will work toward the Greater Good, so that we may best focus upon the immediate matters at hand where we can most directly make a difference. We are best designed to operate upon matters within our own spheres of influence, and to do so most effectively, we must often relinquish control and concern over all that extends so far beyond us. As we exercise our faith in accomplishing these smaller things, it will be strong and resilient when needed in confronting greater issues.

Faith is a form of courage by which we, as conscious entities empowered by our Maker, will act to the best of our capacity. By proceeding with life in good Faith, we will achieve our best possible results in the best possible manner. Additionally, we will preserve faith so that when we may fail, we are not defeated. With courage, we will adjust, and on successive attempts become more adapted to our goals, forms, and ideals.

And beyond what we can control, and when our 'best' is exhausted and seems to be 'not good enough', we can have faith in *all* that is greater than us – for the Greater Consciousness is relentless, unstoppable, and will ultimately prevail with all that truly *is* best.

In these ways, and many more, it is best to have a simple yet immeasurable faith in all that is good – for the domain of the Greater Good extends far beyond what we can observe, comprehend, or control. Then in the overcoming of fear and worry, accept all that happens, even if events occur which are apparently against our best deliberate efforts. This does not necessarily mean that our efforts are wrong or in vain, but there are times when we must reflect, redirect, or regroup. And yes, there will be times when we feel confounded, and in some situations, it is best to simply accept. Accept that what is best will eventually prevail.

In this manner of acceptance, we are never accepting defeat in any form. It is simply that we are confirming via Faith, that our Joy, our Life-force, and our Love, are not lesser things than any problems, setbacks, or defeats that we may encounter along our respective ways.

Fear, the opposite of Faith, is like a void that may never completely go away. But Faith exists squarely in the face of fear, just as light defies the darkness, and Life defies the void of nothingness.

Faith is the courage that comes from the knowledge and acknowledgment of all good things which boldly and truly exist.

Courage, via Faith in all good things, allows us to persevere and *prevail* despite fear.

Supple Like Water

God, you are elusive like a sip of water.
The remembrance of which is misty and vague.
And you have made me supple like water.
And nimble like rabbit.
Alert, cat-like, I sense your world keenly.

The air I breathe does not sting my lungs.
The light does not burn my eyes.
The thoughts in my head do not outright make me crazy.
The sleep each night does not end in not-waking-death.

For these 'simple' things, I am grateful, and many more I shall surely enumerate. Not as an enumerative obsession or exercise, but to be sure to be mindful and grateful for all that is wondrous in this world as I am in it.

A TALE OF TWO RIVERS

Here is the simplest day-to-day philosophy for making choices, a method that may help when making decisions in matters great and small...

At any juncture in life, consider your role in making choices about what to do and what to think about, and even *how* you are thinking about it.

Imagine yourself each day, and during each activity or thought process, as a person who is going to go swimming. Perhaps you are bringing your family, all clad in their swimwear, along for a nice swim in a river.

The allegory here is that we 'swim' within our activities, thoughts, emotions, and our overall attitudes.

Here is the simple part to consider at any juncture:

There are two rivers.

Basically, you can choose to take yourself and your family swimming in a normal, healthy, pleasant, and reasonably clean river of Life.

Or you can choose to swim in a river filled with sludge, slime, purification, and other toxic pollution.

Either river is just as easy to find. They are both nearby and accessible.

Day by day, moment by moment, at each juncture, which river are you choosing?

Astonishingly, many have chosen and continue to choose to swim in the toxic waters – over and over again.

A SIMPLE PRAYER

God, you are the Almighty, the most awesome, and the most amazing. You have made the way for all things that can be. You have made the way for all good things which are, and all greater things which will be. The universe reflects your unparalleled brilliance, and the future holds vast potential far beyond my wildest dreams. I await with eagerness the grandeur of your newest plans and endeavors, yet unbeknownst to me!

You fill my soul with your untold power.

My hand is steadied by your calming confidence.

My heart warmed by your radiant love.

My mind is quickened by your infinite knowledge.

My sensitivity is sharpened by your encompassing awareness.

My judgment is balanced within your benevolent wisdom.

All that I am is within the way you have made for all things, and I shall bear my role in that place with great honor and a sense of excitement and joy. What a grand miracle is each day, each moment; that I exist within this time and place!

LAST EPOCH

Alive, and talking with the wind.
Breathe, and taste the air again.
Forgetting what you have never known.

So distant, the pull of the stars,
    the height of all heights,
        the farther than far.

So distant, the pull of all stars,
    the higher than high,
        the farther than far.

Singing to the once-old forest
the rivers once called new.
While the whisper that surrounds us -
    Spell bound us.

And the rain that left here yesterday
    is last epoch's morning dew.

One Chance

On high, smile upon me.
Create another day.
One chance, you light the way.

Tell me the story
where all of this revolves
and everything is solved.

And tell me the story
where I can tell you
I can smile on me.

One chance is all it took.
One chance is all it takes.
One chance may come tomorrow.
One chance is here to stay.

For we are only human,
Yet Life is deep and wide.

A Prayer of Asking

Some believe that it is selfish to pray for oneself, for gain, or for improvement. On the contrary, I believe God loves the prayers related to the very specific things for which we are longing. That fundamental aspect of consciousness specifically resonates with those things that we *truly* want or desire. Prayers of passion, concerning the things we are *honestly* most passionate about, are perhaps the most meaningful and effective. That which is near and dear to our hearts will always resonate more strongly with intent and purpose.

In other words, it is best to pray honestly and without restraint for those things that you truly want, or those things which matter *to you* the most. In fact, it is psychologically healthy to release these desires to the cosmos and to ask that the powers greater than ourselves assist us in pursuing and obtaining that which we fairly desire. The desires of your heart are in some ways derived from or inherently planted there by God via our natural experiences. So, acknowledging them, if wholesome and non-harmful to oneself or others, is totally acceptable and worthwhile.

The following is a simple example of this type of prayer of asking:

Hallowed God of all the Ages,

It is always your option and prerogative to destroy me or change me at any time and by any means. In the meanwhile, I boldly ask that you give unto me a deep and residing happiness along with unmarred health, always, and that I live forever. And also, to be wealthy. These and other blessings I ask upon myself and all others as it pleases you.

Thank you for making it OK to feel wonderful!

Thank you for making it wonderful to be awesome!

Blessed is your entire creation,

Amen

A Life-Changing Psalm
of Affirmation

After asking for anything in a prayer, such as in the "Prayer of Asking" above, it is best to follow that prayer on subsequent days with related prayers of *affirmation*. Avoid repeating the prayer of *asking* too frequently, as this suggests a lack of belief in its fulfillment. Instead, reiterate a related prayer of affirmation to confirm our belief that the initial prayer *is already in the process of being answered*. This serves as an affirmation of our confidence in the ultimate fulfillment of our bold and heartfelt prayer of asking.

Whether used following a prayer of asking or independently of anything previously asked, an affirmative psalm or prayer is of great effect and can bring a calming sense of peace. This type of prayer is basically a psalm of thankfulness. When we affirm in this manner, we can more fully release our attachment to the outcome. This allows us to be more permeable and accepting of the *way* in which the outcome will come into play. Growing and expanding beyond our own rigidity is an inherent part of the process. The growth and enlightenment we experience may turn out to be as valuable (or more valuable) than that which we had originally sought.

Here is a simple and honestly stated affirmation that has helped me become more appreciative and receptive to all that is good in my life. If this prayer only deepened my sense of appreciation, then that alone would be a worthwhile success. If it additionally alleviated some of my worry, concern, or attachment to the subject matters of the prayer, then that would be an additional boon. On top of these 'internal' benefits, it is said that affirmations of this type literally enhance or hasten the attainment of the goal regarding the subject matter being affirmed, not merely our appreciation of those things.

Another goal of such affirmations, even when the goals of these affirmations are not yet fully reached, is to expand our capacity to believe with confidence in our limitless boundaries concerning all that is possible, credible, and apt to become reality.

Even beyond our 'limitless' boundaries, we may rest assured in the confidence that God may exercise all power and capacity on our behalf.

For surely, God loves our prayers and vibes of affirmation and appreciation.

Life is great!

I am alive and healthy, feeling good in every way, and staying active.

I am happy, without serious reservation, and elevating that state always.

Wealthy as much as needed, and then some.

In a good relationship with my best friend - the creator and sustainer of the universe. Amazing!

Having good relations generally with family, friends, and associates.

Planning to live forever, in spirit, by Your grace - and in body, along with science, by staying active and healthy.

My accomplishments in life are, on the whole, for the good, and with a little good luck – and if it is within Your will – may the sum of my actions be for the greater good, as these are my sincere intentions.

My progeny will be bountiful and blessed.

And therefore, I mourn for no small issues or distractions, as all issues and distractions are quite small in my sight now.

Correctly feeling this way, I shall not feel that I *have* to do anything, and all activities and actions are of my own free will, not of compulsion nor borne of gaining and losing ideas.

In this way too, by allowing a place for the goodness of Life to thrive within myself, may the influence of that which is greater than myself shine through in my actions.

And I will not fret over the lack of anything, nor the state of things, for my own state is very good, and worthwhile, and not to be thwarted by lesser concerns.

And I am eternally thankful to the awesome Eternal Consciousness for granting all of these things.

May he similarly bless all others as they too deserve.

Of Time, I Shall Have It

Of time,
I shall have it,
In limitless quantities.

Of joy,
I shall revel deeply
within.

Of vitality,
I will be un-surpassing
in strength.

Of riches,
In vastness, I shall sit
unaccountable.

Thus, did my spirit speak in thanksgiving,
and so may each of us freely do.

WHEN ERRORS OCCUR

When we encounter a problem, error, or transgression – especially if it is of our own making – the best response is to take the following steps:

Acknowledge - Feel Remorse - Apologize - Make Efforts to Amend - Forgive

To acknowledge, we must recognize and accept what has occurred and any potential ramifications.

If no harm was done, it is not a real problem of any significance. But when harm has been done, even if only in emotion or psyche, we should feel remorse appropriate to the level of damage. But in doing so, never in extreme beyond our capability to bear. Our remorse over any incident should never be in a manner or fashion that creates further damage to another or oneself. The remorse should be remedial in nature and intent. Any degree of remorse that only creates more problems is non-productive and excessive.

From our sincere feelings of remorse (feeling genuinely sorry), we should express this sentiment verbally for ourselves or on behalf of the offending party. The apology will ideally express our understanding of the event, its causes, and the extent and ramifications of the harm done.

Most importantly, attempt to devise and implement a plan that will undo or remedy the harm and prevent this type of error in the future. This step involves making efforts to amend the situation, which may take considerable time and effort in some circumstances. It may take days, weeks, months, or even years. In some cases, the harm done in certain types of disasters can never be fully undone.

Then forgive yourself (if you were the offender), or forgive the others (whoever caused or contributed to the problem), and finally forgive Reality and by extension the Maker (especially where no humans were at fault). For all things may be seen as arising ultimately from God, and as such, all errors belong to him. He takes responsibility for all yet forgives all, so in turn, He should be likewise forgiven. The creation and governance of a universe may not be as simple as it appears, so we must observe grace, forgiveness, and understanding.

Even in events where you were not the cause, and even for events for which no human was at fault, it is legitimate to follow these steps on behalf of the reality to which you belong.

Yes, this means that if a tidal wave occurs, you may acknowledge it in all its tragedy. Feel an appropriate level of remorse (without allowing remorse to do further harm to yourself or others). Then apologize on behalf of nature or perhaps for the flawed or sometimes brutal nature of Reality. Express your heartfelt sorrow to any victims or persons who were injured or inconvenienced. Then begin to do what you can to help make whatever amends are possible or feasible. Help to ensure that the damage from future events of this type might be mitigated. Finally, forgive those who have offended or caused the issue, especially when the offense was unintentional and non-habitual.

In some cases, the amendments may require *sincere* character changes from the offenders, or limitations to be imposed upon them. The Master of Reality will surely reflect kindly upon our remorse and more so upon our just efforts, and in time, will incorporate our good and conscious desires into the whole of the unfolding Pan-Reality.

Following these steps is one way that we, individually and collectively, can improve the human condition and the very nature of reality.

Forgiving God, Mankind, and Self

In order:

Forgive God (and all his creation).

Forgive Mankind (and all of its people).

Forgive Yourself.

For the former have committed the greatest of sins and calamities.

But remember, they have also created the *far greater good* as well.

An astonishing world and universe have been built, against which our societies do not compare.

A great civilization has been built in this world against which we, as individuals, do not compare.

 The New Mythologies

So, knowing this:

Love God (and all of his creation).

Love Mankind (and all of its people, and the good results of their efforts),

and Love Yourself.

For while not perfect, all are from one and share one fate.

All are worthy of respect, love, and awe.

A Work in Progress

God is that all-encompassing existence which miraculously yet absolutely defies the impossibility of existence.

By this definition, God's existence is inherently certain.

The act of Creation is a work in progress, and not a work of absolute perfection.

Yes, magnificent beyond our comprehension.

Far more good than bad, but not without flaw.

Not without room to grow and improve - and it will,

In ways that will exceed our wildest expectations.

The Song of Joy

The short summary:

If I *had to* boil everything down, my best single piece of inspirational advice is…

> ***Keep a song of joy in your heart.***

Of course, we can't literally "boil everything down" to just one thing – even though our rational minds would like us to do so. Life is just not that simple or one-dimensional. Obviously, there will be *many* other principles that one would additionally wish to follow, and there will be many other goals and pursuits toward which we would wish to apply our best practices and principles.

Along the way to achieving our goals and living our best lives, there will be setbacks and even tragedies. But through it all, as much as possible, remember to keep the *song* and the *joy* alive.

What is this '*song*'?

Well, it does not have to be a literal song, although thinking about playing a favorite tune in your mind *can* be part of it. This 'song' is the *song of joy*; a joyful essence that flows through time, the way a real song flows through time. It flows like a river. It can be an underlying current to one's state of being.

The song of joy can reside in the background of whatever you are doing, and it may follow you wherever you may go. At other times, this 'song' may exist more in the foreground and thereby it can more fully occupy your conscious 'state of mind'.

The Song of Joy Flows Like a River.

One might say it is like a mood, an emotion, or a feeling, but it is much more than that. For this 'river' of 'joy' can carry you *through* the many moods, emotions, and feelings that may arise. If you have a loss, and a naturally accompanying feeling of sadness, the river of joy can persist alongside the sadness for a while. Diminishing the loss, it may be what carries you *through*. It does not drown out all feelings and emotions, but it does tend to dampen all our negative emotions, washing them away sooner and more cleanly.

It prevents neither great tragedies nor simple concerns from arising, but it can clean away the toxic residues deposited by these events. We can always be restored to a clean and whole state by the river of joy. For as we know, time heals all wounds, and swimming in this river of joy hastens or quickens this process.

We all know of events or hurtful feelings that once seemed overpowering, but now, after months or years have passed, seem trivial. Perhaps now we might even look back and smile or chuckle in amusement. The river, the song, are your allies in these matters.

The song of joy tends to produce more happy emotions and positive moods, but it is not *just* an emotion or a mood. Like so many attributes of the deeper innermost realms, it can be difficult to define. But it is so very important. So, let us try…

What is Joy?

Some might ask, so perhaps we should start with, "What is Joy?"

The answer is both straightforward and elusive, for how could someone explain joy to another who had never experienced it? An explanation of this type would be like trying to explain colors to a person who had been blind from birth. Yet there is an underlying assumption that *all* of us have experienced joy in some way, shape, or form. While this assumption is most likely valid, there may be some value in pursuing the exercise of attempting to further elucidate the topic. Perhaps by way of reflection, symbolism, or illustrative verbal narrative, we may come to grasp the very nature of joy more clearly.

Certainly, you have experienced joy if you are not a robot, but some of us might have to pause to recall and recollect the emotion. For some of us, pure joy was more common when we were children. But even then, the sense of raw joy was perhaps momentary and fleeting. As we age, these moments sometimes seem few and far between. But joy can be regained, but we must often listen quietly for its song first. Its gentle cadence may perhaps be heard above the din as if beckoning from a distance.

We must find a way to draw nearer to it, or to bring *it* closer to our hearts and minds. We might need to 'practice humming' (figuratively speaking) this song of joy for a while before it becomes habitually stronger. Listen for the sound of the running waters when lost in the forest, and then you can follow the stream to your safe destination.

The apparent distance between us and this song may be seen as indirectly fortuitous. For while a child has no knowledge or control over the coming and going of the song of joy, as we become older and wiser, we recognize that we *can* and *do* have some role in this. In this way, it can become more prevalent and steadier within us. So the song is like a medium by which the state of joy can be perpetuated. It is like a system or process over which joy may be sustained and strengthened.

One way to understand joy is to imagine stripping away all thoughts and feelings for a moment. You now have a default and very neutral state of being – just you, without any noise. Many would say this state is good, and some would contend that we should learn to become content in this default 'empty' state of being. But this quiet contentment is *not* joy.

From this default empty state of 'contentment,' we are now absent from all distractions – like still water with no ripples. Now, out of all the thousands of possible thoughts or feelings, take one small step toward something positive. This small positive step, in the absence of all else, represents joy. That fundamental goodness of being that can and does exist can be expressed in the absence of distraction and even in contrast to, or against a backdrop of, potential negativity.

A gospel song that was popular in the once impoverished rural regions of America says, "Keep on the sunny side of life." This is a literal song that expresses the concept and tone of 'the song of joy'. Many people who appreciate this song have experienced the dark side of life (abject poverty, great sorrow, or disastrous tragedy) and thereby realize the importance of the song of joy on a personal level. In this and many other examples, it seems ironic that by enduring adversity we are often given great strength and wisdom. It is ironic that our sense of joy and its importance is often realized in the very midst of true hardship.

The more one abides within this song of joy, the fewer negative thoughts and emotions one will find. Similarly, if you feel a lack of joy, you may notice that your mind is dominated by negative thoughts and emotions. Left unchecked, these negative emotions may distance us further from the capacity for the simple recognition of joy. The river of joy becomes harder to find, and the song of joy becomes fainter and more difficult to hear. It is still there but so far off in the distance as to be almost indiscernible.

So, first, try to let go of negative thoughts and feelings while cultivating positive 'vibes'. This can be a simple way to strengthen inner joy or at least prepare a fertile place for the joy of Life to take root.

Some feel that it is difficult or impossible to 'get rid of' their negative thoughts. But - *wait a minute* - who controls your mind anyway? Sure, we all have impulses, and I don't think we will ever 'get rid of' all negative thoughts or impulses, but for now, maybe it is time for *a little* self-discipline. Impulses aside, you *do* control your own mind, and your feelings often reflect or shadow what you think about or dwell upon. Assuming some personal responsibility is part of this process.

Despite any adverse circumstances you can't control, you do largely control the domain of your mind across all circumstances. This holds true whether you choose to acknowledge it or not. It is true even if you have, to some extent, abdicated the control of your own mind. It remains true even if you refuse to accept the responsibility for your own mental state.

Yet joy is not *merely* the sum of positive thoughts and feelings. Still, having a mindset that is geared toward positive thought will give joy a place to start. Don't be so consumed with negativity and doubt, or you will leave no room for joy to take root and grow. If you are in that seemingly joyless state, it is perhaps time for some 'hard work' and discipline. We can start by 'clearing out the weeds' and giving a place for something more fruitful to grow.

But let's face it, the so-called 'hard work' of developing a positive mindset is actually *fun*. It is a lot more enjoyable and much easier than the *truly* 'hard work' of groveling in perpetual darkness.

And in the most troubling of times, please recall, *that for some of us*, we are closest to appreciating and understanding joy in our darkest moments of adversity and travail. So, have hope even when all seems lost, for you may be nearest to your own greatest revelation or moment of enlightenment.

Once you have developed some level of positivity, you *will* witness that 'spark' of joy. Like a scout building a campfire with flint and tinder, take notice of this spark and cherish it. Nurture and protect it and do what is needed to make it grow.

Many of these descriptions are symbolic, of course, but perhaps the spark analogy portrays joy as too fragile. So, perhaps comparing the song of joy to a river is more apt.

Consider that first moment of joy as experienced by a negatively shattered soul, as being the first drop of water on the face of a man wandering in a dry and parched land. Taste and cherish that first drop of rain, and smile on the inside, knowing that there *will be* more rain to come.

So, there it is; joy is when you 'smile on the inside'.

Go with it, keep it. Ride the wave. Flow with the river. Sail with the breeze.

Enjoy life, whatever form it happens to take.

Rise up. Straighten your back. ***Smile on the inside***, and don't be *afraid* to smile. Look up at the sky. Breathe in the air. It is OK to be human. It is OK to be you. It is more than OK. You have every right to *be*, and every right to be *you*.

You have every right to be the most awesome version of yourself.

Whether we were created by God or nature, or both, you exist as a living, breathing miracle. The world, with all its feeble aches and moans, is still an incredible and wondrous place. The universe is filled with infinite possibilities. Alas, it is not your path to experience *every* possibility, nor to shrink away from them all, but rather to seize each day and pursue that toward which you are drawn.

But wherever you may go, whatever you may pursue…

do so with a song of joy in your heart.

THE DREAM OF THE MAKER

While sleeping one night, I had a vivid dream wherein somehow…

I was engaged in a very 'hands-on' practical experience, working on a project that required performing a series of manual tasks. The tasks were quite involved and demanded a good degree of dexterity.

In the dream, I was in a large futuristic workshop or assembly room. There, I was fixing a rather elaborate yet broken tool of some sort and then making a new one just like it. The project required some thought and analysis, as well as engaging in the physical process of working on the new version of the complex tool using a range of other simpler tools.

The final tool was quite complex, like nothing I had ever seen, but of course, in my dream, I knew *exactly* what it was. We were planning to make a whole bunch of them.

The dream seemed to go on and on. I recall that I was thinking a lot, even while working on the futuristic devices which were of vital importance.

Later in that dream, the experience of being something (or someone) that can make something, and then making something that can be used to make something else, somehow gave me a revelation concerning man's true relationship to God.

This 'realization' occurred *within* the dream as I was working on the tools but remained with me after I awoke.

The Realization of the Maker's Dream:

We are designed to act within and interact with this world.

We are equipped with consciousness for vision and understanding, a mind with which to think clearly, and hands with which to act precisely.

God's gift, his miracle, is the *never-ending now* and *the nature of the reality* in which we reside. He animates it moment by moment and makes it such that we may choose among many paths and accomplish many great things... or not.

In fact, he *wants* us to make choices and decisions... and to *engage with* reality.

He is *not* really so restrictive, and instead, has laid out a literal plethora of possibilities before us. Beyond the manifold 'ordinary' possibilities reside an array of *heightened* opportunities, which we have yet to imagine.

For us, the meaning is to let go and listen to our hearts – our inner voice. This inner voice may be akin to God's voice. But more importantly, we are to use our instincts and reasoning to make choices boldly, to forge ahead, and to *extend* the greatness of His reality. This is the reality that lives within and amongst all people, including the society of mankind, and the natural world in which we reside.

Choose and act boldly within this construct provided by the Creator, for what within it has he not made possible?

Also, quite simply, immerse and indulge in His great reality. The purpose of Life, in one simple respect, *is to live*.

If the purpose of life is to live, we should certainly do it well.

Have a Grain of Faith

So, stop being overly distrustful of Life and Reality.

Have a grain of Faith.

Don't be overly concerned with mere survival or mundane issues.

Don't be overly fearful over anything or everything that "might" happen.

Rest in the Faith that the Almighty Maker and his Reality *will* provide, and especially so if we reside in Faith.

See and enjoy the phenomenal joy and beauty of creation, more deeply and more often.

Do not always see through tainted, jaded eyes.

Appreciate *Life* and soar while you may with a euphoric, glowing soul.

THE PHYSICAL AND THE SPIRITUAL

I believe that I now see life more closely to the way it is; as a biological process that supports and services a conscious spiritual process.

Perhaps the spiritual process gave rise to the physical process, or perhaps it is the other way around. Either way, this may be a "which came first, the chicken or the egg" type of conundrum.

The order of it all may not matter, and to us, it may not be knowable. It doesn't matter.

But it *does* matter that we recognize *today* that the physical form of life seemingly both *yields* and *serves* a more elusively complex, yet more essential, spiritual process.

The entire physical universe, and our bodies which have arisen from it, serve to facilitate and support our consciousness - a very uniquely aware conscious process.

The body both yields and serves the conscious mind.

The physical world both yields and serves Greater Consciousness.

We cannot really know if the physical world somehow arose as a construct of a primordial Consciousness. However, we *can* see pretty clearly that the physical world (including our physical bodies) serves and supports our more complex forms of awareness and spirit, which are so vital, outstanding, and exquisite.

THE STITCHER

You are the stitcher, the thread, the cloth, and the weaver of time.

Sustaining us in each moment, and skillfully stitching each moment together.

Amazing are you, Timeless One, in that even the nature of my own thought is not possible without you – the foundation, the very form of consciousness.

And yet subtle and unassuming, I might live my lifetime unaware of you.

In your grace, you neither demand nor force my attention.

The New Mythologies

But you faithfully hold all of Reality together, unseen
by my eye.

And among the many possible ways you have made,

You provide a *way* for happiness to thrive within Life.

For all these things, I am happy and grateful,

Always and forever,

Amen.

The Angel's Prayer of Protection

Though the fate of every angel is sealed, the fate of man is less certain.

God, please bless and protect these wonderful, fragile beings.

www.ingramcontent.com/pod-product-compliance
Lightning Source LLC
Chambersburg PA
CBHW042100150726
48005CB00033B/1275